ARRESTING ABORTION:
PRACTICAL WAYS
TO SAVE UNBORN CHILDREN

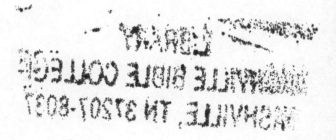

ARRESTING ABORTION:
Practical Ways to Save Unborn Children

THE RUTHERFORD INSTITUTE REPORT: VOLUME 4

by
John W. Whitehead
Franky Schaeffer
D. James Kennedy
Melinda Delahoyde
Joseph M. Scheidler
David N. O'Steen
Darla St. Martin
Marilyn Lewis

Edited by
John W. Whitehead

CROSSWAY BOOKS   WESTCHESTER, ILLINOIS
A DIVISION OF GOOD NEWS PUBLISHERS

 # 1230830 9

Note: This book is not intended to be, and does not constitute, the
giving of legal advice. Particular court decisions may not apply to
particular factual situations, or may not be legally binding in particular jurisdictions. The existence of many unfavorable decisions indicates that reliance should not be placed on the favorable decisions as
necessarily dispositive or assuring victory. This paper is not intended
to substitute for individual reliance on privately retained legal counsel.

To Tom Neuberger,
a faithful friend and supporter over the years

Contents

Editor's Foreword

The most important single issue facing this generation is the devaluation of human life. With over 1.5 million abortions annually and the recurring problem of infanticide, we have reached a crisis point in America. We face, most imminently, the death of our culture.

We have assumed, especially since the rise of the eugenics movement of the 1920s, that we have the awesome authority to deny future generations the right to live. Organizations such as Planned Parenthood are established on the basis that "parents" can *plan away* future people.

But with such assumptions, eventually the concept of who or what people really are was bound to become blurred. Once we play God with who has a right to live, it logically follows that we can play God with who has a right to die. This is especially so if the entity at the beginning of the life spectrum is described as merely "protoplasmic rubbish," "the product of pregnancy," "the conception," "potential life," or in other dehumanizing terms.

Why not apply similar terminology to the infant with Down's syndrome? Why not allow such infants to starve to death? Such was the case with Infant Doe, who in April 1982 was allowed to starve to death because of congenital problems, most of which could have been cured with corrective surgery.

Why not pull the plug on the "clump of flesh" that was once affectionately called Grandma? Are we so naive to believe this does not happen at least with some regularity in medical centers throughout the United States?

As traditional values have waned, we have seen our

entire culture shift to a relativistic view of all things, even life. As our society has bought the secularistic concept that it is the here and now that counts, the idea of a future (and especially of future generations) has faded. *Posterity has become passé.*

This is clearly reflected in recent statistics which indicate that the leading form of birth control is now sterilization.[1] Imagine it: a significant portion of this generation no longer has the option of childbirth.

This trend, along with the entire secular matrix, indicates the death of our culture. Not only do we kill our children, but now we cancel them out completely.

Arresting Abortion
Although our culture may have a denigrating view of people, in recent years there are those who have come to the forefront to fight for the dignity of people.

A new tide of Christian activism, under the leadership of such people as the contributors in this book, is seeking to rebut the dehumanization monolith. As these numbers grow, we are seeing a renewed emphasis on the dignity and worth of people. This has led to creative attempts to save those children, unborn and born, who fall under the death shadow of the surgeon's scalpel.

The rise of Christian activism has afforded methods to arrest abortion. Many of the practical ways to stop abortion are included in this book.

Read and study these essays. Commit yourself to stopping the heinous crime of abortion. Be willing to stand firm before what is surely the bloody face of history.

Finally let us, no matter our religious or philosophical persuasion, join hands to end the atrocity of abortion. This is the task before us. Let us dutifully attend to it.

John W. Whitehead
Manassas, Virginia

Acknowledgments

I would like to take this opportunity to thank all the people who made this volume possible.

The authors of the various chapters worked under short deadlines. Their cooperation is appreciated.

Rebecca Beane, my administrative assistant, was very helpful. Without her assistance on details, this book would not be what it is.

The support of my staff at the Rutherford Institute and my wife, Carol, and five children was important in bringing this volume together. Also important was the encouragement of friends such as Franky Schaeffer, Jim Buchfuehrer, and Tom Neuberger. I am appreciative as well for Toni Mayer's typing of the manuscript.

Finally, my greatest appreciation goes to all of those people who are providing practical ways to save unborn children. Abortion is *the* most important issue today, and it is people such as this who are the real heroes of the present.

John W. Whitehead
Manassas, Virginia

PART ONE:
The Problem

1
Decision Time
by Franky Schaeffer

When Doctor C. Everett Koop, Francis Schaeffer, and I toured the United States some years ago to launch our film series, *Whatever Happened to the Human Race?*[1] one of the reactions we generated from Christians who came to our seminar/premieres was incredulity and disbelief. This disbelief was in regard to claims being made by us that abortion would open the door to infanticide—the killing of a child who has been born—and that, in fact, infanticide was already rampant and spreading as a means of dealing with children deemed to be defective in one way or another. Our seminars were before the well-publicized Infant Doe and Baby Jane Doe cases.[2] At that time, infanticide was strictly being practiced under wraps and without much publicity from any quarter except scholarly journals such as the *New England Journal of Medicine*,[3] which had already printed one or two proinfanticide pieces.

Abortion, once unthinkable, had become thinkable. *It had also become legal.*[4] At that time we were predicting that the unthinkable idea of widespread infanticide as a means of "treating" unwanted born children was becoming thinkable and soon would become legal. This assertion was borne out by facts some years later, and nowhere more dramatically than in the Infant Doe case in Bloomington, Indiana, in which that child had care and feeding, as well as liquids, removed from

3

him and was starved for six days before he finally died. All of this with the legal sanction of the courts of Indiana![5]

Following that evil event, the Department of Health and Human Services (now under the leadership of the Reagan administration, Mrs. Margaret Heckler, and Dr. C. Everett Koop) tried to introduce measures that would curb the growth of infanticide.[6] These were met with near unanimous opposition from the American Medical Association, lawyer's groups, civil libertarians, and other pseudo-liberal elements which make up the leadership in the medical, ethical, and legal fields in our country.[7]

Apparently we had indeed arrived at a point at which the unthinkable proposal of infanticide was moving into the preserve of the thinkable and the legal. This was true to the extent that the law was letting the medical profession know that it would not interfere to prevent the medical profession from exercising its "best judgment" on who should live and who should die, based on a quality of life quotient.[8]

The sad litany of the "progress" made by the infanticide movement in America goes something like this: In 1972, an infant was starved to death at Johns Hopkins Hospital because it had Down's syndrome. An "experimental," "progressive" documentary was made in a re-creation of this event.[9] In 1973, a prominent pediatrician revealed that 14 percent of the infant deaths at the Yale-New Haven Hospital were caused deliberately.[10] In 1976, seventeen of twenty-eight eminent bioethicists said in a medical journal article that killing the handicapped child is sometimes acceptable.[11] In 1977, nearly three-quarters of pediatric surgeons, answering a survey, said they would not act to save a mentally retarded child.[12] In 1982, Infant Doe was starved to death in Bloomington, Indiana. In 1983, Baby Jane Doe was denied surgery in New York. In 1984, physicians in Oklahoma explained how they chose twenty-four spina bifida babies for an early death based on a quality of life quotient.[13]

The important thing to note here is that none of the doctors or lawyers involved in these cases (which present only a tip of the iceberg of children who are victims of infanticide) have been prosecuted for murder or even had their licenses revoked. Infanticide, therefore, for all practical purposes, is legal in the United States today. *Infanticide is being widely practiced.*

Ideas Have Consequences: The Christian Failure

Ideas can therefore be seen to have had brutal consequences. The mentality of abortion, that of ridding ourselves by killing the unwanted unborn child, has now spread to the born infant. The unthinkable has become the thinkable.

Unfortunately, and most tragically of all, the unthinkable has also become the thinkable for many who call themselves Bible-believing Christians. Evangelical leaders and other Christians, long silent on the abortion holocaust and refusing to get their hands dirty and do something about it, have also refused to involve themselves with the infanticide cases.[14]

While there has been scattered protest, it has been from individuals, not in any sense from the evangelical establishment. This is in contrast to the Roman Catholic university hierarchy that has been vocal and consistent in its opposition to abortion and infanticide.[15]

Moreover, there seems to be a growing number of evangelical leaders who, not content merely with passive acquiescence, are actually contributing to the problem by reviving the eugenics movement. InterVarsity Press, for example, published a book called *Brave New People* (now available from Eerdmans) by Gareth Jones which argued for "therapeutic" abortion and left the door wide open to both genetic engineering and genetic screening for defective infants.[16] This book, amazingly enough, was endorsed by a number of leaders of the Protestant evangelical establishment. This Christian book endorses the use of amniocentesis *for Christian couples* in order to find out if their child is defective, so they can abort that child.[17] This is the infanticide mentality.

In another book by Carl F. H. Henry, titled *The Christian Mindset in a Secular Society*, Henry argues that some children can be aborted if they are seen to be so severely handicapped that they do not, in his opinion, evidence the image of God![18] In another book, Letha Scanzoni argues for abortion if someone even *suspects* that she is going to have a defective child because of contracting rubella during pregnancy![19]

The thing to note here is that all of these ideas come from reputable bastions of evangelicaldom. All of the authors, especially Carl F. H. Henry, as well as the publishers in all three cases, once had reputations for upholding orthodox, conservative, evangelical Christianity.

Such acquiescence to the evil winds of change around us today can only be seen in the light of the same kind of acquiescence that the church made in the face of the Nazi holocaust. Then silent churchmen did nothing to stem the tides of Nazism, and some churchmen even spoke in favor of it. Similar also was the attitude of many naive churchmen in the 1930s who, like the Dean of Canterbury, found excuses for and even approved Stalin's harsh and brutal methods of controlling the Soviet Union.[20]

We can see, therefore, that acquiescence to the pressures of the day, the desire to be fashionable and at the "center of things,"[21] is nothing new, as far as Christians capitulating before social pressures. However, in our time we are responsible to do something about the pressures we face. That there were Christians who held slaves and endorsed slavery on a "biblical basis," much as Carl Henry now endorses "therapeutic" abortion on the basis of who is or who is not created in the image of

God, is no excuse for us to do nothing about the plight of those who are being stripped of their human rights today.

A Tragedy in the Making

The continuing insensitivity of the evangelical leadership and many evangelical individuals to the problems of abortion and now infanticide, with euthanasia looming on the horizon,[22] is a tragedy. This acquiescence to evil will lead to tremendously negative results which include: (1) the continuing loss of life of 1.5 million unborn children a year; (2) the growing number of infanticide cases, many of which go unreported since virtually no one cares; (3) the hardening and desensitizing of the Christian conscience in this country to the point that there will be nothing left to appeal to; (4) the eventual full-fledged revival of the eugenics movement[23] in which the right to life is based only on one's capacity to "contribute effectively" to his society; (5) the eventual persecution of the faithful within the church, since those who stand up against such monstrous oppressors will be increasingly singled out as unwanted, just as the unborn is unwanted today (we already see the beginnings of this when "the separation of church and state" argument is used to muzzle Christian opinion); (6) the loss of human rights and freedom in the United States in other areas of our lives (besides abortion and infanticide), for if one can be stripped of the very right of life for reasons of convenience, certainly he or she can be stripped of other rights such as property, liberty, and political rights (also for reasons of mere convenience, privacy, or whatever else the zealous legalistic elite who push for these secularistic changes come up with); (7) the removal of God's blessing from our society and from those individuals who have acquiesced to these monstrous evils; (8) the complete death of the Christian witness in this nation, since to separate personal conscience from public behavior (i.e., "I'm personally against abortion, but I wouldn't impose my views") is to separate the concept that Christianity is *true* in all areas of life from that truth itself, thus leaving us merely with another religion; (9) the continuing upsetting of the population balance in the United States in which an aging unworking population begins to put greater and greater financial pressure on the shrinking working population as abortion and then infanticide, for an increasing number of reasons, begin to eliminate more and more "unwanted" infants.

No Excuses

When we made *Whatever Happened to the Human Race?* there was a general lack of information within the evangelical Bible-believing community as to the reality of abortion and infanticide. There was, one could say, some excuse for the lack of involvement. Now, many years after the making of *Whatever Happened to the Human Race?* there are more than one hundred books on the topic, a growing number of films, hundreds of articles, and journals such as *The Human Life Review,* as well as a whole group of renowned speakers, doctors, scientists, physicians, and politicians who have strongly spoken out on the issue.[24]

Thus, for the evangelical community to still be acquiescent, silent, or, worse, supportive of the abortion industry to one extent or another shows a hardening of conscience that has nothing to do with a lack of information.[25] In other words, there are no excuses, and we are going to have to take full responsibility for our inaction. This includes moral responsibility before God and political responsibility for the loss of freedom for all but an elite in our culture.

In terms of God's righteous anger and judgment, we must bear full responsibility for our inaction in *external terms.* In light of Christian apathy, inactivity, and acquiescence toward the abortion and infanticide industries, one can only tremble and shudder for American

8

Christendom when one reads verses such as those telling us that many will say "Lord, Lord" and our Master will turn to them and say he never knew them. We have indeed turned our back on "the least of these" with the full knowledge that we are doing so, since the facts are now open for everyone to see. We are told that if we do not see, our sin does not remain with us. However, if we say we do see, and yet do nothing about what we see, our sin remains with us. That our culture will be judged and cursed for these actions is certain.

What cannot be proved, but what I believe to be no less certain, is that on Judgment Day many of those arriving saying, "Lord, Lord," considering themselves good evangelicals, may find that they were on the wrong side all along. Heaven is said to contain many surprises. One of them may be how few who call themselves evangelical Christians from the second half of the twentieth century will actually enter the Kingdom on that great day.

Evangelical groups, institutions, and the evangelical establishment in general have been enamored with activities, church growth, expanding magazine circulation, and so forth. We are told in the Bible, however, that God does not want our activities or sacrifices. Instead, he wants our obedience; sacrifice without obedience comes as a stench to God's nostrils. I believe the American evangelical church, its establishment, its leaders, its pastors, and its people, inasmuch as they have done very little for "the least of these" in our day and age, are a stench to God.

Changing Things

One of the things that keeps me from plunging over the line of despair is that I do not believe that anything in history is inevitable. I do believe people can change things. I believe even small minorities can change them. I believe that the activistic minority can change and lead even an apathetic majority. I believe that standing up for something can actually change the direction of history. I do not say that I believe this *will* happen, but I believe that it *can* happen.

Because of this, I think it is not an entirely idle speculation or an exercise in futility to examine here what the results *could be* if evangelicals, including at least some of the evangelical establishment, stood up and began to make the human life issue a priority issue in this nation. Of course, they would have to be willing to pay the price Jesus paid; that is, they might have to become unfashionable, despised, hated, and ridiculed. But that is the price for standing for truth.

Practical Realities
First, let us look at some political ramifications. If the evangelical establishment, its leadership, magazines, academics, and others, were willing to speak with a *united voice* and assert that no Bible-believing Christian in good conscience should vote for, elect, or tolerate any official at any level of government—from the lowest office to the highest—who did not have a clear prolife view, no such officials could be elected.

There are supposedly forty million evangelicals in America. United with strongly principled orthodox Roman Catholics, this bloc would form a majority swing vote that would be absolutely unbeatable in terms of American politics as we know it now. If this bloc of people all registered to vote, and then voted consistently on prolife issues, there would be no officials in government anywhere in the United States of America at any time who would espouse proabortion views.

There would also be no politicians to turn a blind eye to the growing incidence of infanticide or tolerate, in the midst of public discourse, talk of euthanasia for the elderly. There would be no Governor Lamms of Colorado espousing the voluntary euthanasia of the elderly to create, as he put it, the "humus" (compost) out of which the new generation could grow.[26] There would

10

be no possibility of the Democrats nominating the Geraldine Ferraros of this world who aggressively pursued "abortion rights" and at the same time called themselves "religious."[27]

This would mean, however, that we would have to bear the cross of looking "absolutist," "intolerant," "bigoted," "right-wing," and "fanatical"—a cross that Christian academics have been unwilling to shoulder as they pursue fashion and acceptability from an academic elite whom they wish to ape and be patted on the head by (or at least earn their doctorates from).

Stopping Abortion Now

Let us look too at the practical day-to-day reality of abortion, and how to stop this trade in human flesh.

In your average American town or city, the ration of abortion clinics to evangelical churches, let alone Catholic churches, is about one abortion clinic to every one hundred churches. (Consult your phone book if you need proof.) The actual number of people directly involved in the abortion industry is probably no more than approximately twenty thousand nationwide. (This would include abortionists, nurses, administrators, owners of clinics, and those who manufacture abortion equipment or dispose of the dead babies.)

There are, however, said to be forty million evangelicals in the United States. Obviously, the fact that evangelicals have not changed the situation on a neighborhood-by-neighborhood, town-by-town, county-by-county, and state-by-state basis reveals that they do not really want to. Evidently if even a small percentage of the total number of evangelicals would regularly picket abortion clinics, indulge in sidewalk counseling, be willing to be arrested during sit-ins, and express other public displays of godly civil disobedience (nonviolent in nature but effective), the abortion industry would close its doors within a week.

Any abortion clinic which is unpicketed in an area

11

in which there are evangelical Christians—in other words, every town in America—is a clinic that has, figuratively speaking, a seal of approval on the door which reads: "This clinic owned and operated with the blessing of the evangelical community." The silence and lack of picketers in front of that clinic speak volumes. Any town in which the local jail does not on a daily basis have evangelical Christians being thrown into it for having sit-ins and disrupting the abortion business in nonviolent but principled ways is a jail over whose door could be inscribed: "You don't have to bear your cross here."

There are many areas in which abortion clinics are actually operated on the same block as, next to, or even across from an evangelical church. And yet many of these churches in direct contact with abortion clinics do not have any outward sign, or inward sign for that matter, that they will provide an alternative to the women whose lives are going to be shattered by murdering their babies.

If every evangelical church in America felt a sense of mission to care for "the least of these," there would be very few abortions. If every church provided a crisis pregnancy center or teamed up with another church to do so, put sidewalk counselors outside of abortion clinics on a round-the-clock business-day basis as a mission to the needy, provided love and care for the pregnant women, and at the same time picketed the abortion clinic to a standstill, there would be very few abortions performed (whether abortion was sanctioned as "legal" or not). That this is the case is proved by the success at stopping abortion that such groups as the Pro-Life Action League, under the direction of Joseph Scheidler, have had.

Modern Christianity is derelict in these important life and death matters. This can be seen by the fact that modern Christianity is not consistently using the political clout it has—that it is not voting in a bloc on prolife issues, or putting the heat on from the grass-roots level on up, or picketing, opening crisis pregnancy centers, and in other ways stopping the evil abortion industry dead in its tracks.

Even in smaller, less dramatic ways apathy is rampant. It amazes me that Christian women (and their husbands) do not even take the trouble' to find out if their gynecologists do abortions. It amazes me that they use hospitals in which abortions are performed.

Many Christians take their wives to hospitals in which the room in which their baby is delivered and taken home for a Christian baptism is the same room in which only moments earlier a child's life was brutally taken through dismemberment, poisoning, salting out, and other foul means of the abortion industry—a veritable death chamber no less! This is no better than their using a gas chamber at Auschwitz in 1944 for church services during the SS's lunch break! If Bible-believing Christians would refuse to use a medical facility that housed either an abortion clinic, an abortionist, or in which abortions were performed, the medical industry, forced merely through its shrinking pocketbook, would be reduced to rubble or have to change its tolerance of abortion. This could be done with minor inconvenience—merely driving to another hospital across town, or changing doctors. But do evangelicals even do this? The answer unfortunately is often no.

What to Do

There is no doubt in my mind that if even only a significant minority within the evangelical bloc would act consistently on the ideas expressed in this Rutherford Report, including those mentioned here in my own essay, the abortion industry could be brought to a standstill and politically disenfranchised through evangelicals voting as a consistent bloc (no more proabortion government officials at any level). There could also be a change in public perception because Christians would be willing to go to prison for standing against the abortion industry through means of civil disobedience that were nonviolent and therefore acceptable (just as the nonviolent civil rights movement was acceptable). Confronted by a militant church that took its faith seriously enough to make sacrifices for the truth, abortion could be stopped as a common legalized practice in America, and the advance of infanticide blocked.

Modern Christians, however, have not used the means available to stop abortion. In fact, they have not even had the courage to speak out against abortion.[28]

It is instructive that at the time of this writing, a leading evangelical magazine such as *Christianity Today* has never even had a cover story on infanticide. In the eleven years since the legalization of abortion in *Roe v Wade*, *Christianity Today* has run *one* cover story on the topic of the prolife movement (a 1983 article entitled "Why Prolife Rhetoric is not Enough"), and not even one on abortion itself! *Christianity Today* covers news of abortion, pickets, protests, and so forth (buried deep within their news section), while it editorializes at great length on other more fashionable problems of our day and age which are mere footnotes to this central concern. Thus, the sins of omission have been as grave as the sins of commission, perpetrated by those such as Carl F. H. Henry who have to one degree or another left the door open to abortion by favoring some part of it.[29]

Conclusion

Let me conclude then by listing some priority measures that need to be taken immediately.

(1) Christians must speak out against their own evangelical leadership within the evangelical establishment who refuse to take a stand. We must try to convince that leadership, and if they cannot be convinced replace them. This means protesting magazines like *Christianity Today* which will not make this a priority

14

issue. This means not inviting those such as Carl F. H. Henry to speak at our organizations because they take a view that abortion is permissible on handicapped children who, in some cases, are not considered to be created in the image of God. This means supporting those within our churches that *will* take a stand on these issues, and firing those that will not. This is tough talk, but abortion and infanticide are life and death issues.

Things have gone so far within modern Christendom in the refusal to take a stand that at times they become absurd. Wheaton College has a philosophy professor, Arthur Holmes, who has endorsed the book *Brave New People* with its proabortion views.[30] It has an ethics professor who spends time looking for excuses for "therapeutic" abortions in his so-called "ethics" classes, rather than standing against the practice of abortion universally. And yet Wheaton College will not hire a professor who refuses to sign a pledge not to drink or smoke! The lesson here is that apparently drinking and smoking are priority issues, but abortion is not.

This type of evangelical absurdity must be changed, reversed, and rescinded. Abortion must be made a priority issue, and if the church leaders, the university leaders, the academicians, and the magazine editors in the evangelical community will not change their views, we must replace them, disenfranchise them, and find other authentic *Christian* leaders. Then and then only will the church resemble anything of what it should be. Monstrous evil cannot be condoned, nor can those who will not oppose it. They are false teachers.

(2) Having begun, as the saying goes, "to clean up our act," we can then turn our attention to the abortion industry itself. We cannot wait for Washington, D.C. or our local politicians alone to solve the problems for us. Indeed, the more we actively do, the more likely we are to keep the issue on the front burner so that the politicians will address it also.

Direct action in our communities is necessary. This

must involve round-the-clock picketing of abortion clinics; acts of peaceful, nonviolent civil disobedience; carefully planned strategies to provide compassionate, complete care for women who elect not to have abortions— as well as for their babies; the establishment of pregnancy centers; and an escalating campaign that will give this society a choice to either lock up thousands of Christians in prison (because of sit-ins, etc.) or address this issue. If at any given moment several thousand Christians are serving time for sit-ins and other acts of civil disobedience, that will bring the abortion industry to a standstill. If several thousand more cases are on court dockets, and if several thousand arrests are being made weekly, you can be *sure* that the issue *will be* on the front burner, and our nation will have to deal with it.

(3) We must keep the heat on through political channels. This means that, as listed in point 2 above, we must take direct action on a community basis.

In addition, we must vote consistently as a bloc on this issue. We must agree that no matter what other issues we have disagreements on, whether they be issues of defense, foreign aid, or other public policy debates, we must *all* agree on this one issue. We will not elect candidates who are not clearly prolife and willing to do something to change *Roe v. Wade.* And we will actively fight against candidates who are proabortion or even undecided or uncommitted on the issue.

Only such stern resolve will change this issue. You cannot do everything at once, solve all the world's problems, and take care of every human need. However, if we would all unite on this one issue, we could do two things. We could change the abortion practice and industry as we know it, thus stopping the rise of the neo-Nazi eugenics movement.[31] Moreover, we could send a clear message to the secularist zealots in this nation that we refuse, as a Christian people, to simply bow out and turn our whole society over to them.

16

Abandoning Pietism and Fashion

For these things to happen, we must abandon two things: (1) the pietism which we hold so dear that separates our "personal spiritual lives" from our "public everyday lives"; and (2) the idea that we must be fashionable and acceptable at any cost.[32]

Pietism is death and signals the end of the concept of Christian truth and absolutes. If one can say that his personal morality dictates one thing but he's going to act differently in public on issues such as abortion,[33] then what he is really saying is that his personal morality is worthless and absurd.

Fashion is also death. The Bible and the church hold up hero after hero and teaching after teaching telling us that we should buck the trend of a society when it is wrong, not go along with it.

If we can abandon these two false gods of pietism (in other words, feeling nice but doing nothing) and fashionability, then we can perhaps do something to stop the slaughter of innocent children. In the word "perhaps" there is both hope and despair. Perhaps we can, but perhaps we will not. God has at times chosen to show his mercy by moving the hearts, minds, and souls of enough Christians (at the same time) to change great evils and to send a fragrant incense to heaven that signifies obedience.

Let us start by praying for such a godly zeal to descend on our leaders and on ourselves. Then let us not sit back and do nothing *but* pray. Let us instead act—act for change, act vigorously, act courageously. And as we hope to see God's mercy, let us act on behalf of "the least of these."

2
Myths and Realities
by D. James Kennedy

Before I formed thee in the belly, I knew thee; and
before thou camest forth out of the womb, I sanctified
thee, and I ordained thee a prophet unto the nations.
(Jeremiah 1:5, KJV)

Abortion is the most important single moral issue of our
time. It has been called by numerous writers "the
American holocaust." This topic deals with a matter of
vast importance. It deals with the matter of life and
death.

The Declaration of Independence says: ". . . We
hold these truths to be self-evident, that all men are
created equal, that they are endowed by their Creator
with certain inalienable Rights, that among these are
Life, Liberty, and the Pursuit of Happiness." More important than liberty, more important than the pursuit of
happiness, more important than economics, and more
important even than religious freedom is the question of
life itself. If we are deprived of life, then obviously all of
our other rights are gone as well.

Since the famous *Roe v. Wade* decision in 1973, sixteen million unborn babies have been killed. That number is greater than those lost in all of the wars that have
been fought in the history of America. Obviously it is a
problem of tremendous dimensions.

Whose Problem Is It?

What kind of problem is it? Is it a political problem? Well, it obviously has a political aspect to it. But *it is basically a moral problem,* an ethical problem, a spiritual problem, a biblical problem. There are well over a hundred texts in the Bible dealing with this subject. It is a subject about which the Bible has much to say. However, all too often we have been silent even as many were silent in Germany when the great atrocities were taking place there.

Who are the people that are involved? There are some who say it is merely a woman's issue. I have great sympathy and empathy for a woman, especially a woman who, out of wedlock, finds herself carrying an illegitimate child. Like others, I feel empathically toward her and am concerned for her plight, so much so that we have started a home through our church to try and provide a positive, viable alternative to abortion—a place where women and their babies can be cared and provided for.

However, this is not merely a woman's issue. There are others concerned as well, including, for example, the husband. That newly created life is as much the husband's as it is the wife's. Historically, it is interesting to note that when the Roman Empire did away with laws which allowed abortion, it was done not because of the woman or the harm that abortions were doing to women (and indeed they do do a great deal of harm—vastly more than most people are aware of in this country), but because the husband was being defrauded of his progeny.

There are others that are involved as well, such as grandparents. As the father of a marriage-age daughter, I myself have an interest in her children, as does every other grandfather or grandmother who love their grandchildren. It is also true of siblings. Many people

19

have complained about never having had brothers or sisters with whom to grow up.

Even society has an interest in the death of millions of its citizens. I remember well reading the story about the birth of one baby. The circumstances were so tragic, the poverty so great, the handicaps so numerous that by a half a dozen different standards used today this baby would, no doubt, have been aborted. That baby was Ludwig van Beethoven. I think we have some interest in the fact that that baby was not killed.

But most of all, there is the matter of the child itself. The Bible speaks very strongly about "hands that shed innocent blood" and God's great displeasure with the shedding of innocent blood.

We must also consider God himself. These are creatures made in his image, and he is greatly concerned about them. So there are many people that are involved in this.

Reasons for Abortion
We are told that legalized abortions are much safer than illegal abortions. That, I might say, is contested by people who know the facts. For example, in 1967 there were 275 deaths in this country as a result of abortion. That was when only a few states had legalized abortion. Interestingly, 164 of those deaths were from legal abortions. That was more than the deaths from illegal abortions at that time.

Let's consider some of the other reasons that are given for abortion and consider these rationally. First of all, we are told that abortion is not the killing of a real person, that unborn children are not living human beings, that such are simply the products of conception, that they are simply fetal material, that they are genetic garbage.

Recently, however, sixty prominent physicians met

in Cambridge, Massachusetts, and presented a declaration which said that the biological facts are absolutely conclusive that the unborn child is a living human being. These doctors include Drs. Hofmeister and Schmidt, past presidents of the American College of Obstetrics and Gynecology, and also Dr. Joseph Faley, past president of the American Academy of Neurology. Also included was Dr. Bernard Nathanson, formerly one of the leading abortionists in America, and many other prominent physicians. These doctors said: "The developing fetus is not a sub-human species with a different genetic composition. As clearly demonstrated by *in vitro* (dish) fertilization, so also in *in vivo* (womb), the embryo is alive, human, and unique in the special environmental support required for that stage of human development." That is, the unborn child is a genetically unique human being. This is medically incontrovertible. Every doctor knows this. Every scientist knows that from the moment of conception this is a specially unique, genetically different human being.

I remember listening to a doctor point out that he had talked to dozens of physicians around the country who had performed abortions, and he asked them if they knew that what they were destroying was a human life. Their responses were very interesting. Every one of them, he said, became angry. Why did they get angry? Because they were destroying human life? No. Because his question implied the possibility that they may have been so ignorant that they did *not* know they were destroying human life. They said they were doing it for a good reason.

Every doctor knows what is in the womb! But many women have been deceived by the linguistic gymnastics used to hide what they are doing. Every doctor knows it. They have known it for centuries. The Hippocratic oath, which has been used in Western civilization by doctors for well over two thousand years, makes it very clear that the doctor will give no abortive remedy. It is interesting that now we are returning to a pre-Hippocratic period. There are some medical schools that no longer use the Hippocratic oath for that very reason.

We are also told that women have the right to choose. That is a very interesting thing. It is an aborted sentence—the "right to choose." In our society, it ends rational discussion. It is an emotional declaration. It is a sentence without a predicate. Obviously a moment's reflection would indicate that a person does not have an unlimited right to choose anything that he wants to do. *The very essence of civilization is based upon the limitation of the people's right to choose.* Do I have an absolute right to choose? I am sure that if I went to a meeting of the National Organization of Women (NOW) there would be a resounding vote: "Yes, we all have the right to choose!" Wonderful! I choose to kill you. Do I still have the right to choose? That puts a little different coloring to the question, doesn't it? The ironic thing is that there really is no informed choice given to those women who abort their babies.

A young man who heads up an organization that has been picketing various abortion chambers talked to the owner of one of these places. He said to him (and this man very much objected to this): "If you will just give me a little desk in the corner somewhere inside your place where I can have a few minutes with each of these ladies to explain what the alternative is to abortion and exactly what is taking place in abortion and what that is within her womb, we will immediately stop the picketing." The man's response? "Never! Forget it." The only choice given to the women entering this man's clinic is whether they want the abortion on Tuesday or Saturday. After all, it is only the product of conception. In talking to numerous people who have had abortions, they have told me that never once were they told that

what was inside of them was a baby. It is called everything else but that.

The Semantics of Death

Abortionists use the term *fetus*. Why do they use that
term? Do you know what a fetus is? Do you know what
fetus means? *Fetus* is a perfectly good Latin word. It
simply means an unborn baby. Martin Luther knew how
important it was for the Latin Scriptures to be translated
into the vernacular so people would know what is going
on. And the abortionists know how important it is to
translate the English words into Latin so that young
women won't know what is going on.

We are told that the fetus is not a person. As the
abortionist backs away semantically he says, "Well, yes, it
may be a living human being, but it does not really have
personhood." Now, that certainly dredges up some very
interesting historical reminiscences. For example, it reminds me of 1857 and the Dred Scott Case wherein the
Supreme Court indicated that the black man, the slave,
was not a person. It reminds me of Nazi Germany where
the Nazis maintained that the Jew was not a person. You
see, *these people knew that before you can enslave or extermi-
nate human beings, you have to depersonalize them—dehu-
manize them.* You have to semantically destroy them before you physically destroy them. You have to make
them into something less than human persons. That is
exactly what they did then, and that is what is being
done now.

It is interesting that the same depersonalizing arguments that were used to support abortion were the same
arguments used to support infanticide in the Baby Doe
case—"not a person." They are the same arguments
used to support the destruction of the mentally deficient
or defective babies—not fully "persons." We should never forget that before Adolf Hitler ever killed a single
Jew he murdered 275,000 handicapped people. First,

abortion had been prevalent in Germany for over twenty years; then there was infanticide, the killing of babies; and then there was the destruction of 275,000 adult handicapped people.

Abortion has been prevalent in Japan for decades. What has happened? First, there was a strong push for euthanasia, a strong push to get rid of the elderly and the defective. Why? They destroyed the younger generation, and they have so many older people to support that it is becoming economically infeasible. Therefore, now the economic pressures are causing some to advocate getting rid of the aged. There is a certain poetic justice here. The parents have been killing the children, and now the children are rising up and killing the parents. God will not be mocked!

Not persons, indeed! There are over one hundred biblical texts that make it very clear who they are. Listen to the personal pronouns: "Thou didst clothe *me* with skin and flesh." Clothed what? It? *Me,* with skin and flesh. "And knit *me* together with bonds and sinews."

"Thus says the Lord who made you, who *formed you from the womb* and will help you." "Behold *I* was brought forth in iniquity, and in sin did my mother conceive *me.*" Or, in Jeremiah, "Before I formed you in the womb *I knew you,* and before you were born *I consecrated you.*" "Consecrated you!" We don't consecrate an appendix or a tumor, but a person!

And when Elizabeth heard the greeting of Mary, the *babe leaped in her womb.* "The babe in my womb," said Elizabeth, *"leaped for joy."* It is interesting that one never hears a woman say that the fetus inside her leaped for joy. It is always the "babe." The Greek word is *brephos;* the babe in the womb is the *brephos.* And what does that mean? It is the same term that was used to describe Jesus, the babe lying in a manger, clothed in swaddling clothes. That is a *baby*—not a tumor, but a baby.

The Unwanted Child

We are often told that unborn babies should be aborted because they are not wanted. This, indeed, brings up a very new and interesting perspective on the inalienable right of life. It depends upon some popularity contest. If one is not wanted, then one surely should not be allowed to be born. It is an interesting philosophical and logical twist of things.

Of course we would all agree that it is nice to be wanted, that everybody should be wanted. Certainly every wife has the right to be wanted by her husband. We would all agree with that. If some young lady should come into my office and tell me a tale of woe (as has been done many times before) and say that she is not wanted by her husband and her heart is broken, you know what I would say to her? I would say to her, "My dear, I think that is the saddest thing I have ever heard. It breaks my heart to hear that your husband, that mean old wretch, doesn't want you—a lovely thing like you. Well, there is only one thing to do." I open my drawer and pull out a gun and BANG she is dead. That solves that problem! Bring in the next counselee. Does that not follow from such a fallacious agrument? If her husband does not want her, then there is nothing to do but to kill her. That is so ludicrous, so absurd, so illogical as to be virtually irrational, except that there are millions of people going around saying it: not wanted.

In the case of a baby it is not only irrational, it is also a lie. There are one and a half million abortions performed every year in this country. There are two million couples looking for babies to adopt that they cannot find. Many adoption agencies have had to close down because of a lack of babies. The babies are all in the incinerator. Couples have had to wait five and ten years to get a baby. On the black market today babies are selling for $35,000. I want to tell you this: nobody spends $35,000 for something he does not want very, very much. *Babies are wanted!*

We are also told that because they are not wanted, they will be abused. They won't be abused if they are adopted by people who *do* want them. Of course, again a lie is involved. Here we are told that the basic reason for child abuse is that children are not wanted. Yet, studies have shown that the vast majority of abused children *were* wanted. It is another one of the lies.

Since we have destroyed sixteen million unwanted children, child abuse should virtually have disappeared from America. Yet, it is epidemic in our time.

Why do we have so much child abuse? It is because we have devalued human beings and, in particular, children. We have destroyed them by the millions in the womb. We are now moving toward destroying them after they are born. In the Baby Doe case, one young college-age girl came to a counselor and told the story of years of child abuse in her home. She said that the thing that hurt her most of all was when her mother would say to her, after beating her, "And you just remember that we didn't need to have you at all." Have we sunk so low that the day has come when children will have to get up in the morning and thank their parents for not having killed them? What a distortion of everything decent and moral!

Then we are told that a woman can abort an "unwanted" child because she has a right over her own body. And that is supposed to be so self-evident as to immediately end the discussion. My friends, what shall we say about that? My response to that would be: of course a woman has a right over her own body. Who would dispute such a fact?

We should point out, however, that this right is, by law, limited. A woman does not have the right to commit suicide. That happens to be against the law. But within reason she has a right over her own body.

Thus, the statement is true, but it is totally irrelevant because that baby within her does not happen to be a part of her body. The same sixty prominent physicians, including two past presidents of the American College of Obstetrics and Gynecology, said this also: "A human ovum fertilized by human sperm produces a biologically identifiable human embryo." Thus, it has separate and unique genetic information and biological material. Every cell in a woman's body has exactly the same forty-six chromosomes and exactly identical thousands of genes in those chromosomes. Every single cell is identical in that way except for the cells in that baby. They all have different sets of chromosomes and different sets of genes.

The baby even provides his own nest. Many people do not realize that the baby is the one that creates the placenta. It is the baby that produces the umbilical cord. The baby has its own bloodstream. It has a different blood type and produces its own blood. In half the cases the baby has a different sex.

It is also interesting to see that developments in fetology, the science of the study of the baby (which coincidently began in 1973, the same year *Roe v. Wade* was decided), are producing some amazing revelations. An example is *in vitro* developments. This is the maturation of the egg and sperm in a dish outside the mother. From this, scientists are finding that they can keep that newly created life alive longer and longer before implanting it in a womb. At the same time they are able to cause the baby who is born prematurely to survive at an even younger age. Scientists say that they can keep the embryo alive longer *in vitro* and that they can cause the premature to survive at an earlier and earlier age, and that before the end of this century those two figures are going to meet. Scientifically this says that a baby can be conceived, fertilized, and grow to maturity without ever having been inside the womb of a woman. I personally don't know that that is so desirable, but nevertheless it is scientifically true.

Let's suppose that we go ahead a few years and that comes to pass. There are babies that have been fertilized and conceived, who grow up never having seen the inside of the mother's womb. Is a woman going to say, "Oh, that is just a part of my body"? It will be self-evident that this is a separate, unique, genetic individual, totally apart from her body. That is true! And right now that baby is totally dependent upon her for its nutrition and protection. But does that mean that it is a part of her body? Let me point out to you that when that baby is six weeks old, it is still totally dependent upon the woman for nutrition and protection. Because it is not viable apart from the care of the mother and totally dependent on her, then obviously at six weeks of age (even after birth) the mother also has the right to kill the baby because it "can't survive without me." What about six months? How about a year-old baby? Can he take care of himself? Well, kill him also!

How about a sailor in a submarine? It is submerged for six months, and all the air that he breathes is dependent upon that submarine. So is the food that he eats and the protection from the pressures and the water of the sea. All are dependent upon the submarine. Obviously any intelligent person should be able to see that that sailor is simply a part of the submarine! Well, logic is logic, isn't it?

Rape and Incest and the Devaluation of Women
We are also told that abortions are performed to save the mother's life. Less than 1 percent of all abortions are performed to save a mother's life. That is simply a smoke screen. We are told that when delivering a child to save the mother's life the doctor is doing something altogether different than abortion. He is trying to save both the woman and the baby if that is possible. That is

quite different than having a baby aborted and then, if it survives the abortion procedure, allowing it to die with a sign over it saying: "Nothing by mouth."

What about the matter of rape and incest? These are probably the most difficult things. Again, less than 2 percent of all abortions are done because of rape and incest. It is indeed a very tragic thing, a very violent and evil crime. But how do we solve it? By committing another violent act? By killing the innocent child who is as much a victim of the rape as was the mother and who had, in fact, nothing to do with it at all? Do two wrongs make a right? In the Bible the child of rape was allowed to live and the rapist was put to death. Today we find that the penalties against rape have become more and more lenient, whereas the child is now the subject of a vigilante form of capital punishment. Justice has been totally destroyed and perverted in that the guilty are practically allowed to go free and the innocent are killed. This is the very antithesis of justice!

It is said that women would have abortions even if the law didn't allow them. Is that true? Well, let's look at history. Romania had free abortions for decades. This was so much so that the population rate of growth had sunk so low that the whole economy and future of the nation were jeopardized. Thus, in 1965 Romania passed laws which very strictly limited the number of abortions that could be performed. What happened? In the very next year the birth rate doubled, which is to say that there are many women who will abide by the law even though there are some who will not.

We are told by some of the radical feminists that the women will become hysterical; they will abort themselves with coat hangers; they will go insane; they will commit suicide; they will abuse and perhaps kill their children.

Rosemary Bottcher, an analytical chemist whose major work deals with protecting the environment, says she doesn't like the picture of women the radical feminist abortionists are giving us—that it is a very unflattering picture of women. She doesn't think women are that way at all. And I happen to agree with her. Bottcher says that if that is true, and if women cannot handle the stress and pressures of a pregnancy, how are they going to handle the stress and pressures of the Presidency?

Many feminists become irate (rightly so) at the idea that sexual freedom should be placed in a way that allows men the right to rape women. But they insist that their sexual freedom allows them the right to kill unborn children. Feminists lament men's reluctance to recognize their personhood, but they steadfastly refuse to recognize the personhood of the unborn. And, indeed, I might add that they get most furious at the pornographers and playboy advocates who see women as nothing but meat—flesh on display. At the same time, the feminist insists that the baby is nothing but flesh, tissue, a product of conception.

Rosemary Bottcher says that men are expected to be mature when they conceive a child. They are expected to endure inconvenience and hardship if necessary to provide the means to bring a child up and to send him or her through college today (even if this requires taking an extra job or working late at night). He is supposed to do this because he is mature. The woman, however, according to feminists, is painted as someone who is so selfish and so immature and so irrational and so hysterical that she cannot stand the fact of a few months of inconvenience in order to bring life to another person or to bring happiness, perhaps, to some other family who might adopt that child. I agree with Rosemary Bottcher that that is, indeed, a denigration of the female sex in its entirety. I find that most of the women that I know are rather altruistic. They are concerned about others. They give themselves for others. Indeed, the feminist portrayal of women is something less than flattery, to say the least.

A Time to Stand

My friends, the time has come for Christians to stand up. They need to become active. They need to fight this gross moral evil of our time.

We have seen that there is not a rational argument that can be presented for the flood of abortions which has launched this nation into a sea of blood. God says, "Woe unto the land that sheddeth innocent blood." We are perhaps going to bring down upon us the very wrath of God. I am certain that this hideous blot on the escutcheon of mankind will be wiped away, just as slavery went the way of other evils, and just as the Inquisition passed away. Just as Nazism passed away, so also will this butchery of the innocent pass away. However, it will leave a scar on the historical character of our nation.

May God grant that because of our prayers, our concern, our action, abortion and the other devaluations of life will pass away soon, before many other innocent children are given over to butchers who have no feeling about taking the life of the silent innocent. One of the signs of character and morality is the concern for the weak, the sick, and the helpless. Even as the chivalrous knights were concerned about women, so should we be concerned about these members of our society who are the most helpless, the most silent sufferers in our time. God grant that soon this evil will pass from our land! May it be!

3

Violence and the Prolife Movement

by John W. Whitehead and Franky Schaeffer

Recent bombings of abortion clinics have galvanized proabortion organizations in denouncing what they term are acts of "terrorism."[1] Although it has been alleged that many of these so-called bombings have been carried out by the abortionists themselves (to serve as antiprolife propaganda), it is equally clear that some violence and talk of violence has crept into a small part of the prolife movement.

Those active in the prolife movement must be especially careful not to force the state into the position of prohibiting prolife activities because of violence toward abortionists. We must keep the door open for dissent and protest against abortion, a door that violence would close. (It should be noted, for the record, that it is the abortion industry who, by the violence they commit against the "least of these," the unborn, have unleashed such talk of violence.)

In the United States, under the Constitution, the question should never be "May we dissent?" or "May we oppose the actions of government or individuals?" To the contrary, we not only have the right to dissent, criticize, and oppose, but in some circumstances, such as the question of legalized abortion, we also have a *moral duty* to do so. The Constitution guarantees us this right. Despite zealous secularist efforts to eliminate religious freedoms, great freedoms remain.

The crucial questions concerning the methods of the activist prolife movement are these: "How may we dissent?" and "How should we conduct ourselves when dissenting, opposing, or criticizing the devaluation of human life?" (Before going further, let us note that the principles we espouse here apply only to action within a free and democratic society such as the United States. They do not necessarily apply to how one could or should bring change in a closed totalitarian state such as the Soviet Union.)

The freedom to publicly speak one's mind, to picket, and to otherwise oppose the devaluation of human life is a part of our fundamental law. As former Supreme Court Justice Abe Fortas has written:

> From our earliest history, we have insisted that each of us is and must be free to criticize the government, however brashly; even to advocate overthrow of the government itself. We have insisted upon freedom of speech and of the press and, as the First Amendment to the Constitution puts it, upon "the right of the people peaceably to assemble and to petition the Government for a redress of grievances."[2]

Both *advocacy* and *action* are protected under the Constitution when carried forth peaceably. *Violence, however, is not protected.* Physical attacks upon persons and destruction of property are outside the law. Such should not be condoned and practiced by those seeking meaningful change in *free* governments. Instead, violence and all unrestrained abuses should be condemned or an anarchy could result. This is aptly exemplified in Lebanon and Northern Ireland.

The Biblical View
The first recorded act of human violence in biblical history occurs with the murder of Abel by his brother

Cain, an act of violence which can only be understood in the context of the story of man's fall in Genesis 3. In choosing to stand against his Creator, man not only disrupted his communion with God, but also found himself alienated from his fellow-creatures. Cain's violence was a direct consequence of alienation from the Creator brought on by the Fall—an alienation which has been substantially healed by our redemption through Christ. Despite man's alienation from God, he has the unique status of having been *created in the image of God.* This means that man is a reflection of the Creator, and therefore is a being of great worth and dignity. Violence against human life, including the destruction of a man's property, violates man as he is before God and as he is in himself, and is thus *a violation of the image of God.*

A key to our discussion of violence is the term *destruction,* which had its beginning in the Fall. The Fall was man's attempt to be his own integration point without a reference point in the Creator—that is, to be his own god. Thus, as an attribute of feigned deity, violence (and thus destruction) was a logical necessity of the Fall. Violence is the perverted use of force in man's struggle to usurp the place of God in the scheme of things. For the Christian, such a usurpation of divine authority is forbidden, not being within the biblical framework.

Such usurpation, however, is within the philosophical framework of modern existentialism, which is the attempt of man to play God. Jean-Paul Sartre, for example, said that "Man is the being whose project is to be God."[3] Sartre posits that man "is completely and always free or he is not free at all."[4] Quoting Dostoyevsky, who once wrote, "If God did not exist, everything would be possible,"[5] Sartre claims that this is exactly the starting-point for existentialism: everything is permitted. This includes "freedom" to commit violence.

The implications of man's attempt at being deity in the exercise of violence are far-reaching. When man seeks to be God, he is faced with the problem of the display of power. The prayer of Hannah in 1 Samuel 2:6 sums up two dramatic aspects of God's power: "The Lord killeth, and maketh alive; he bringeth down to the grave, and bringeth up." If man plays at being God, he will, like the abortionist, since he cannot create life, manifest his claim to godhood by destroying or at least abusing life. This is, in essence, the devaluation of human life in humanistic terms.

Understanding Violence

There are various facets of violence, two of which are pertinent to our discussion. The first is the *reciprocity of violence*. In the Garden of Gethsemane Christ said, "All they that take the sword shall perish with the sword" (Matthew 26:52). Christ's statement is an assessment of the reciprocal nature of violence. Violence begets violence and is contagious.

The second facet is the *continuity of violence*. As Os Guinness writes: "Violence may be pragmatically [successful] in overturning an existing order that is corrupt, but it is utopian to imagine that the next order will be free of all such problems."[6] The history of terror that has followed every Marxist revolution testifies to this. Albert Camus in *The Rebel* also concluded: "All modern revolutions have ended in a reinforcement of the power of the State."[7]

George Orwell in his prophetic novel *1984* recognized the corruption of power through violence. The character O'Brien described the future as modern humanistic man would have it:

> Power is inflicting pain. . . . Power is in tearing human minds to pieces. . . . Progress in our world will be progress toward more pain. The old civilizations claimed that they were founded on love and justice. Ours is founded upon hatred. . . . Always . . . there will be the thrill of

victory, the sensation of trampling on an enemy who is helpless. If you want a picture of the future, imagine a boot stamping on a human face—forever.[8]

Violence by those involved in the prolife movement is merely the unwitting continuation and reciprocal infliction of violence begun in the abortion clinic. It is the continuation and extension of the abortionist's initial act of violence—the stamping boot.

Violence, if it were to surface as a significant element, would discredit the prolife movement. The American public will never condone violence of the vigilante type. The proabortion media are already playing on the abortion clinic bombings to portray prolife people as violent. Despite claims by gainsayers, at least moderate progress has been made by the use of peaceful protest in slowing the rate of abortions and in organizing prolife groups. If random violence becomes an intrinsic part of the prolife movement, the American public, as Harold O. J. Brown points out, will welcome force and violence on behalf of the state to stop it.[9] Thus, the reciprocity and continuity of violence will be played out before our eyes in discrediting the prolife struggle, one of the most positive forces in American society.

The Nonviolence of the Civil Rights Movement
The civil rights movement would never have succeeded if Martin Luther King had resorted to violence. Those who advocated violence, such as H. Rap Brown, were hunted as common criminals and with public approval. The black protesters of the civil rights movement found sanction from the very system they were attacking because of their peaceful composure and nonviolence. This is reflected in the courtroom battles that resulted in some of the United States Supreme Court civil rights cases.

One such case, *Edwards v. South Carolina,*[10] serves as

an example of how to affect the system through nonviolence. On March 2, 1961, nearly two hundred blacks gathered at Zion Baptist Church in Columbia, South Carolina. From there, carrying placards and picket signs, they marched without incident to the state capitol grounds to express their grievances "to the citizens of South Carolina, along with the Legislative Bodies of South Carolina."[11] The objective of the demonstration was to protest the ill treatment of black citizens. Supreme Court Justice Potter Stewart describéd the situation:

> As they entered [the Capitol grounds] they were told by the law enforcement officials that they had a right as a citizen to go through the State House grounds, as any other citizen has, as long as they were peaceful. During the next half hour or 45 minutes, the[y] . . . walked in single file or two abreast in an orderly way through the grounds.[12]

The picketers peaceably assembled and expressed their grievances. Not until they were told by the police to disband did they do more. As Justice Stewart wrote: "Even then, they but sang patriotic and religious songs after one of their leaders had delivered a religious harangue. *There was no violence or threat of violence on their part, or on the apart of . . . the crowd.*"[13] The protesters, because of their refusal to disband, were all charged with a "breach of the peace." The mass arrest of 179 blacks was challenged in court. The South Carolina Supreme Court, however, upheld the arrests.

On appeal, the United States Supreme Court overturned the validity of the arrests. The Supreme Court stated that the "circumstances in this case reflect an exercise of these basic consitutional rights in their most pristine and classic form."[14] As such, the acts of the demonstrators were protected by the United States Constitution. The language of the Supreme Court makes clear that the success of the people revolved around their nonviolent posture. This lesson from the past must not be forgotten.

Force Is Not Always Violence

One important distinction, however, must be drawn from the situation involving the black demonstrators in Columbia, South Carolina. Although they acted nonviolently, they used *nonviolent force.* Two principles must be observed in the use of nonviolent force. First, there must be a legitimate basis for and exercise of force. Second, any overreaction crosses the line from force to violence.

What Should We Do Then?

Besides legislative efforts and political involvement, both of which are important, Christians can directly affect abortion in other ways. We must use the "open windows," as Francis Schaeffer called them, to curb and hopefully to end legalized abortion and infanticide. At the least, the number of babies killed can be reduced.

Christian Love

The church should be the first place a pregnant woman approaches for help. Churches can operate or contribute to crisis pregnancy centers. A telephone hotline can be installed and used to counsel and assist pregnant women. Assistance with open homes during and after birth, until the woman is able to function on her own, should be available. Counselors in the church must be prepared to deal with the emotional, psychological, and physical problems faced by women who are being pressured to have abortions. These women need to know there are alternatives to abortion (such as adoption). They also need to know there is a large body of people standing by, ready to provide life-saving alternatives.

Picketing to Stop Abortionists

Picketing is the most effective way to reduce the number of abortions. Some local churches use their Sunday school buses to pick up and drive their people to abortion clinics to picket them. Counseling women as they enter abortion clinics and also guiding them to a local church-operated crisis pregnancy center have effectively deterred women from having an abortion and guided them to a better alternative. Of course, it is vital to approach an abortion-minded woman in a compassionate and nonderogatory manner in order to be heard and to have any influence.

Picketing also serves the important function of bringing the issue of abortion to public light in a nonviolent way. This, coupled with the loss of business, is the reason abortion clinics and abortionists abhor and even fight picketing. Therefore, it must be done *within legal bounds.* Acquire the necessary permit from local authorities, and avoid labeling abortionists, by name, as "murderers" or the like. Such labeling, though true, has resulted in libel and slander suits and is not tactically necessary. Be "wise as serpents," and *think* through your methods *before* you start.

Standing Against Complacency

Methods of nonviolent force should be used simultaneously. For example, a church that operates a crisis pregnancy center can organize picketing and at the same time work for prolife political candidates. We can also stand against the tide in our own Christian groups, refuting those who accommodate the proabortion world spirit in the way many within mainstream Christianity have done. Such undermining of the biblical view of the sanctity of life must be exposed and denounced as antihuman as well as antibiblical. Proabortion views have no place within the church.

Against the Grain

The twentieth century has mainly demonstrated a spirit of violence, revolution, and anarchy. This is reflected in the writings of philosophers of violence such as Frantz Fanon, who writes in his book *The Wretched of the Earth:* "Violence is a cleansing force. It frees the native from inferiority complex and his despair and inaction; it makes him fearless and restores his self-respect."[15] Chairman Mao Tse-tung advocated that power comes from the barrel of a gun. Stalin and others who preceded him, as well as present-day tyrants such as the Soviet government, all promote violence as a solution. As a consequence, millions of people have been tortured, maimed, and killed in our century.

Revolutions have resulted in police states erected to restore order and continue the violence. Violence is the ultimate result of humanism. Without the checks and balances of Christian absolutes (one such absolute being the sacredness of human life), the only thing remaining is raw force. Christians can never submit to violence.

Conclusion

In closing, let us summarize our position. Indiscriminate violence carried on by individuals to bring political and social change in a society often leads to worse circumstances, not better. *Random* violence is prohibited by Scripture as a means to bring political change in a *democratic* society in which we have other nonviolent avenues clearly open to us.

However, we are *not* saying that the Bible always prohibits the use of physical force. We feel that Scripture clearly teaches that the state is allowed to use force, as in a policeman arresting a criminal and putting him in jail, to protect its citizens. We feel that physical force can be used legitimately to defend one's person or family from attack in self-defense. We also feel that the state can use force to defend itself against outside military attack, and therefore our statement here should *not* be misconstrued in any way to be an argument for pacifism. However, the state using force as mandated by God to defend its population against evil attack or crime is a completely different issue from the individual within a society using random violence to right wrongs as he or she sees fit.

In the books of Samuel, David had a very legitimate grievance against King Saul, the head of the state, and had an opportunity to kill him. Recognizing the authority of the King, David chose not to perpetrate random political violence to right his own grievances, however justified. Yet we also see David as a soldier, and later as King, blessed by God when using military force against the Philistines and the other enemies of Israel on behalf of the state or as the head of the state.

Thus, to be against the use of personal violence to right the social wrongs as we see them, and yet at the same time to believe in the *legitimate* use of force, is not in any sense a contradiction in terms. It is only a question of what is appropriate and what the Bible teaches. It is the difference between a lynch mob and a fair, orderly court of law. The abortionist lynches innocent babies without any due process of law. Our answer must be to stop the abortionist, not via another lynching, but by peaceful means. We are defending the due process of law which the abortionist and the courts have renounced.

(The question of fighting state tyranny once a democracy becomes totalitarian, or after an invasion as in China or Afghanistan today, is again another topic altogether. With all other avenues closed, the Christian *might* in good conscience become a freedom fighter or a member of the resistance.)

Under the United States Constitution we have the freedom to picket, march, demonstate, distribute leaflets, sidewalk counsel, write letters, and vote. The Christian community has not yet made adequate use of the avenues open within the limits of the law. *While these avenues remain open, we are derelict in our duties if we do not use them to the fullest.*

But we are also derelict if we overstep the bounds of those freedoms as provided by our Constitution. Not because it in itself is a sacred document, but because we are commanded to be good citizens until such time as we are ordered by the law and government to do those things contrary to the law of God.

Let us therefore unite to fight this great battle, but let us fight it in a biblical way. In a free nation random violence is counterproductive. It is also wrong. And it could very easily discredit all the positive things the pro-life movement has brought forth.

PART TWO:
Solution

4
Infanticide
by Melinda Delahoyde

It has been almost twelve years since the United States Supreme Court gave us abortion on demand in America. Abortion remains the number one moral issue of our day. It is an issue that just will not go away. Yet now we find ourselves fighting the battle for human life on two fronts. Infanticide—the intentional killing of an infant—has come to America. Now not only do we find ourselves fighting for the lives of innocent unborn children, but we must also face the fact that in some of the finest hospitals in our country some handicapped children are denied treatment, some literally starved to death, because doctors and parents think their lives are not worth living. As Francis Schaeffer so often reminded us, the unthinkable has become thinkable.

The Unthinkable
Although infanticide has been happening for years in America, the majority of us only recently learned of its reality. It was in 1982 that the infamous case of Baby Doe in Bloomington, Indiana first awakened the nation to the horror of infanticide. Infant Doe was a baby boy born with Down's syndrome, a common, although certainly not life-threatening, handicap. At birth, the baby required a routine operation to correct a blocked esophagus. Had the baby been "normal," there is no doubt the surgery would have been performed. But he had Down's

syndrome, and so Baby Doe's parents decided against surgery for their child.

Not only was lifesaving surgery denied, but food and water were taken away from the tiny infant. Seven days later Baby Doe died of starvation in the Bloomington hospital. In an article that appeared in *Human Life Review* a doctor described Baby Doe's last few hours:

> Baby Doe's shrunken, thin little body with dry cyanotic skin, extremely dehydrated, breathing shallowly and irregularly, lay passively on fresh hospital linens. Blood was running from a mouth too dry to close. Death by starvation was near. Too late for fluid. Too late for surgery. Too late for justice.[1]

A year earlier in Danville, Illinois Siamese twins had been born to a doctor and his wife. At the twins' birth, their father reportedly signaled the physicians that oxygen was not to be given to the baby boys. Someone also ordered that no food or water be given. The boys were transferred to the hospital nursery and would have starved to death had it not been for an anonymous call placed to state child protection authorities. The babies were transferred to another hospital, and the parents and doctor were indicted for attempted murder. Those charges were later dropped when a nurse could not conclusively link the parents to the order not to feed. Today, much to everyone's surprise, the twins have been separated and are progressing well. What appeared to be a hopeless case, and one in which death was the best "treatment option," has turned out to have a happy ending.

Infanticide is not always looked upon with horror—especially by some doctors. In 1983 several doctors at the Oklahoma Health Sciences Center in Oklahoma City published the results of their work with children with spina bifida.[2] This handicap results when a child's spine fails to properly form in the womb. The degree of mental and physical handicap varies greatly from case to case, and many children experience no mental retardation at all. Prompt treatment almost always results in benefits to the children. In fact, doctors at Children's Memorial Hospital in Chicago have decided that every child deserves treatment since doctors cannot tell who will and will not benefit.

Yet doctors in Oklahoma City had decided that some children did not deserve any treatment at all. They applied a "quality of life" formula to each child's case and determined if the child's natural endowments, together with the family's ability to care for their baby, added up to a high enough quality of life for the child. If the baby "measured up," the child received treatment. If not, the infant was transferred to the home and left to die.

Reporters visiting this home for untreated children found unsanitary conditions, overcrowding, and almost no appropriate medical care. From 1977 to 1982 thirty-three babies with spina bifida were recommended for nontreatment. Twenty-four of them died—most within thirty-seven days. Over one-third of these children with spina bifida who had been recommended to the hospital died during this five-year period.

It is important to note here that many of these children were not born dying. They had every chance to live, but were denied life because parents or doctors thought their life was not worth living.

It really should be no surprise to us that the infanticide issue has come out of the shadows of the newborn nursery. As early as 1973 some of our best philosophers and ethicists were warning us that abortion was only the beginning. Once we allow the casual destruction of some human lives, we open the door for the planned killing of any member of the human community who does not measure up to our expectations or standard of perfection.

There is an undeniably logical link between abortion and infanticide. If we say that a human life can be destroyed three days before birth because it does not "measure up," because it is inconvenient, or handicapped, what is to stop us from taking that same life three days after birth? There is no logical reason not to kill the child. Its life remains inconvenient, and the handicap is now fully visible for all to see. The only real difference is that the baby has been born.

Before birth we call the killing abortion; after birth we call it infanticide. The reasons that we use to justify abortion will also justify infanticide. Although many said it could never happen here, it *has* happened here. Some handicapped infants are killed simply because someone thinks their lives have no meaning.

The United States Supreme Court left the door open to just this kind of thinking in their 1973 *Roe v. Wade* abortion decision. Even though the court maintained that born children are entitled to the rights and protection of our laws, they denied personhood and protection to the unborn. Unborn children, even though they were biologically human beings, did not possess some of the human qualities that full-grown adults exhibit. They were only "potential" persons and therefore could be denied the full protection of our laws. For the first time since the Court passed down their decision on slavery, a class of human beings was excluded from the human family because it did not possess certain qualities.

But if the unborn do not possess certain qualities of full humanity, neither do certain other human beings, such as the handicapped and the elderly. Of course, they are *biologically* human beings, but that just is not enough anymore.

This question of what is a true person is vitally important. Once we begin to separate biological personhood from other human qualities—once we begin to say it is not enough to simply be created a human being—and begin to impose our own standards of "humanhood" on other persons, we have opened up the door to mass human destruction. Of course, the unborn child is human life, but it is only a potential person, they say. Of course, a handicapped infant is *biologically* human, but socially and intellectually it is only a "vegetable." No one—the handicapped, the elderly, or even the socially undesirable—is safe from death.

This is just the kind of logic the Court opened up in their abortion decisions, and today we see the fruit of that logic in the destruction of handicapped newborn babies. One of the best examples of just how far this *logic of death* has progressed in our country is seen in two editorial commentaries that appeared in leading medical journals. The first, written in 1973, appeared in *California Medicine.* The authors acknowledged that abortion killed human beings and that society took such pains to justify this killing with euphemistic language solely because it had accepted the idea that some human lives were not worth living. It was a very honest look at the cheapness of human life in a proabortion culture.

Ten years later *Pediatrics,* the leading journal for pediatricians, publicized a similar commentary. Only this time the subject was newborn human life. In the author's own words:

> If we compare a severely defective human infant with a dog or a pig . . . we will find the non-human to have superior capacities. . . . Only the fact that the defective infant is a member of the species *Homo sapiens* leads it to be treated differently from the dog or pig. But species membership alone is not relevant. . . . If we can put aside the obsolete and erroneous notion of the sanctity of all

human life, we may start to look at human life as it really is: at the quality of life that each human being has or can attain.[3]

The death process began with abortion, but soon progressed to infanticide. In ten short years we had gone from abortion in only the "hard cases" to justifying the deaths of newborn children because they could not measure up to dogs and pigs.

Indeed, it was in 1973, the same year that abortion on demand was legalized, that two doctors at Yale-New Haven Hospital in Connecticut documented the deaths of forty-three infants in the newborn intensive care nursery.[4] All of those babies died because of *intentional* decisions on the part of doctors and parents to deny treatment to the infants. For some of those children there was no appropriate remedial treatment. They were literally born dying, and nothing could be done to save them. Yet many of those babies had every chance to live, though they had life-threatening conditions that needed to be corrected.

The doctors reported that they did not base their decisions on medical factors alone. Parents' desires played a major part in deciding which children lived and died. The result was that many children who had every chance for a hopeful, meaningful life never made it home from the special care nursery.

The evidence that infanticide is happening is overwhelming. Although many believed that such a thing would never happen here, once the logical link between abortion and infanticide was set in motion, it was only a matter of time before it would be happening here. *Abortion led to infanticide.*

The similarities between abortion and infanticide do not end with the logic that justifies both practices. Infanticide advocates have adopted many of the arguments used by proabortionists to justify the killing of newborn infants. For those of us who have been fighting for life, it is no surprise to see the same words and phrases employed in a new context to rationalize a new kind of killing.

If we are going to effectively end infanticide in America, we must unmask these arguments and clearly state our principles of care and compassion. Let's look at the arguments of the proinfanticide forces in our society.

Hard Cases Make Bad Law

In the abortion issue we saw initially that abortion advocates refused to talk about abortion on demand. Even though it was clear that they sought abortion for any reason, they publicly spoke only of the "hard cases"— abortion for rape, incest, or gross fetal deformity. These cases were thrown in the faces of prolife advocates over and over again. We were asked how we could "force" an innocent woman to subject herself to carrying this child to term. Surely that was too much pain for the mother to bear. How could we "force" women to bear children in a situation where they had no choice?

From the way in which these hard-case arguments were framed, one would assume that the only abortions performed were for these most difficult cases. In fact, less than 3 percent of the total abortions performed are for the "hard cases." Yet today we have an abortion rate of 1.5 million children each year. One in three pregnancies ends in abortion, and very, very few of those abortions are performed for reasons of rape or incest.

The hard case, as Harold O. J. Brown commented, became the "convenience case," and abortion on demand became the law of the land. The hard cases were the wedge in the door to allow women to kill their unborn child for whatever reason they chose.

Now we see this same kind of argument being raised in the infanticide debate. Infanticide advocates point to the case of the child born with gross physical and mental handicaps who will require twenty-four hours a day attention from parents and family. Supposedly the child will never achieve any "meaningful interaction." Again the question is thrown back at us. How could we sentence this child and family to a life of heartache and pain for the sake of a child who may never be aware of its own existence?

No one denies that this is a tragic situation, nor that it is very rare. Neither can it be denied that raising a handicapped child poses special burdens and stresses for a family. But once again we must maintain that *killing is never compassionate.*

Even in this most difficult situation, the child is an independent human being, fully protected under the law. No matter how hopeless the situation may seem, killing an innocent child is never the answer. The medical principles of providing care always apply, and our efforts are to be directed toward providing care and life-giving support *for the child and the family.*

As Christians, we must be very careful we do not adopt the utopian, perfectionist thinking of the world around us. Even the most severely handicapped infant is a special person in the eyes of God. God's image is not taken away from children because they cannot do certain things or because they do not possess a certain "quality of life." The life of the most affected child can be a glorious success in God's eyes. It is this kind of life-giving attitude of hope that we must convey to the world around us. In God's view there is no "worst-case scenario." His love and power extend to every human being.

Infanticide advocates, however, deliberately pull out the worst-case scenarios to make us think that these are the only cases in which they advocate death. They want us to think that it is only when there is no hope for family and child that nontreatment is the answer. But, in fact, there are very few of these "worst cases," and when we look at the children who are being denied treatment, they are anything but hopeless cases. Children born with Down's syndrome and spina bifida, who have every chance for a meaningful, hopeful life, are being denied treatment simply because they have a handicap.

We have already progressed far beyond the worst-case phase when it comes to killing handicapped children. If we give in to this "hard-case" argument of the proinfanticide forces in this country, we can be sure that legalized infanticide on demand will be the result.

Complex Issues and Agonizing Decisions

For years those of us involved in the prolife struggle have heard the charge that we were "absolutists." We did not understand the complexities of the abortion issue and the many facets of making the decision to kill a child. Very rarely would abortion advocates come right out and say they advocated killing unborn children. More often they would begin their remarks with a statement about how complex and agonizing the whole situation could be. After those words were spoken, what invariably followed was a defense of legalized abortion on demand. Their remarks about the complexity of it all were intended to make us think that there really are no right answers on the issue.

It was also so complex and perplexing that no one should have the right to decide for another person, they claimed. Only the mother-to-be was able to decide to kill her baby. Complexity was a smoke screen raised by pro-abortionists and intended to make us drop our guard and agree with them that "There really are no right answers here."

Now we see exactly the same argument being raised with ever greater force in the infanticide debate. Infanticide advocates focus on the worst-case scenario of a severely handicapped child and the burdens that this child will cause for family and friends. Perhaps there are no resources within the community to assist the child.

The parents may be financially unable to pay for their child's care. Maybe there is another child in the family who already demands extra attention from the parents.

The situation appears to be so complex that no one could presume, we are told, to impose his value judgments on these parents. The family must be free to decide which is the most important value for them. Perhaps other children in the family are more important to them than the continued care of their new child.

These are "difficult and agonizing decisions." However, the point for those pushing infanticide is that there are no right answers. The child's life is never taken to be an absolute value. It is only one of several values to be considered in the decision-making process.

For some families, financial considerations rank higher than their child's right to live, and they decide against treatment for their baby. For other parents, their child's life comes first no matter what the cost may be to them. The important point, again we are told, is that no law or group of persons should ever tell the parents how to decide. The complexity of the issue makes it impossible for anyone to "impose his morality" on this issue. There should be no laws to protect newborn children, and every case should be handled on an individual basis. After all, as Representative Geraldine Ferraro said in a House debate on infanticide, there just are no "right answers."

But the fact is that there are many right answers in this difficult situation. In fact, there are several principles of action that apply in every treatment decision involving a handicapped child.

The first is that the handicapped child is a fully-protected individual under the law. The parents may not fully value their child's life, but the law does place a tremendous value on that life. He is protected in exactly the same way as a "normal," full-grown adult in American society. The law does not allow parents or doctors to decide that their family's emotional or financial well-being will come before their child's life. The law protects the right to life of every handicapped child, no matter how severely handicapped.

Secondly, doctors are qualified to make medical decisions, but not quality of life judgments about their patients. When dealing with a situation involving a handicapped infant, the only decisions to be made by doctors are medical decisions based on their best medical judgments about the child's condition and prognosis. If an accepted medical treatment is available for the child, then that treatment must be given. No doctor can withhold treatment from a child because he thinks the life is not worth living. It is important to remember that we are talking here about a child who is not born dying. No doctor can be forced to give futile or useless treatment, and no treatment need be given if it is either unavailable or the child's case is medically hopeless and nothing can be done to improve his or her condition.

However, what we have happening in our country is doctors making treatment decisions that are not based on their medical judgments. When Infant Doe was born in Bloomington, Indiana, there was no question that the best medical treatment for the child was an operation to enable him to ingest food. The infant had a life-threatening condition, and the almost always successful operation could remove that condition. But surgery was denied this baby because the baby had Down's syndrome, and because the parents believed the child would have a low quality of life.

Lifesaving treatment was denied Baby Doe because of a quality of life judgment. There is no doubt in anyone's mind that if Baby Doe been a "normal" child, the surgery would have been immediately performed. *We must insist that doctors stay within their area of expertise and not venture out on the slippery slope of quality of life value judgments.*

In the case of any child *we must always insist upon equal treatment* for handicapped and nonhandicapped infants. Legally and ethically we must insist that children should not be discriminated against because they have a handicap. If the treatment would be given to a non-affected child, then it must also be given to the handicapped child. If no treatment is available or it is a medically hopeless situation, then no treatment need be given. It simply does not matter if the child is handicapped.

This is exactly the type of reasoning the Reagan Administration and Congress used when they recently enacted tougher anti-infanticide regulations. *Infanticide is a civil rights issue*—a deadly form of discrimination against the handicapped. Since the mid-1960s our laws have prohibited such discrimination, and now those same laws should be enforced to provide equal protection for handicapped newborn infants. Every infant, no matter how severely handicapped, is entitled to equal protection under our legal system.

What then do we say to those who claim the infanticide issue is too complex to decide? We say that every child is protected under the law and is entitled to equal treatment under the law. As doctors and parents enter into the decision-making process, we demand that doctors stay within the area of their medical expertise and not venture into subjective value judgments about the child's quality of life. With these principles in mind, we can be sure that decisions for treatment or nontreatment of handicapped infants are made with the infant's best interests in mind and do not take us further down the slippery slide of planned human destruction.

Parents' Rights
By far the most powerful weapon in the proinfanticide arsenal is the parental rights argument. Dr. Raymond Duff at Yale-New Haven Hospital very clearly presented this argument in an article in 1973:

We believe the burden of decision-making must be borne by families . . . because they are most familiar with the respective situations. Since families must primarily live with and are most affected by the decisions, it therefore appears that society and health professionals should provide only general guidelines for decision-making. Moreover, since variations between situations are so great, and the situations themselves so complex, it follows that much latitude in decision-making should be expected and tolerated.[5]

Once again the parents' rights argument used in infanticide is a clear extension of the same type of logic used in the abortion debate. The United States Supreme Court gave the pregnant woman an almost absolute right to privacy that included the right to abort her child. If a woman can have that kind of power over her unborn child, the argument goes, then why shouldn't parents have that same authority over their newborn child? After all, it is the family who will be forced to "bear the burden" of raising a handicapped child. Surely the child's fate should rest in the parents' hands.

Of all the arguments proposed by infanticide advocates, this is the most emotionally compelling to many people. There is no doubt that raising a handicapped child poses special problems to be faced. Divorce and severe emotional stress are common in families of special children. To the outsider looking on, and sometimes to family members themselves, death would have been the easier, and therefore the better, course.

However emotionally appealing such reasoning may be, the parents' rights theory does not stand up in law or logic. Our laws recognize a strong tradition of parental rights because society generally assumes that parents would act in the best interests of their child. Parents are presumed to act in the best interests of their child, and as long as they do so, the courts protect their authority.

Yet, many times the courts have acted against parents' wishes when they thought the rights of the child were being violated. In several cases judges have ordered medical treatment for children, including handicapped children, against the wishes of parents. They reasoned that children were legally entitled to accepted medical treatment and that no one would decide that life, including life with a handicap, was worse than no life at all.

A child is not simply a piece of baggage that belongs to the parent. Children are independent persons under the law and entitled to the law's protection. That is why traditionally our courts have ruled in favor of the child when the bonds of parental love and care have been broken.

The courts have maintained this protection for very good reasons. Once we begin to say that a child is not covered by our laws, where do we draw the line? When we begin to reason that life with a handicap is worse than no life at all, who is safe from death? A society that fails to extend legal protection to all children opens the door to selective killing.

Imagine also the kind of perverted logic that would prevail if the child's right to life was handed wholesale over to the parents. Today in our country a pregnant woman can determine through amniocentesis if her child is affected with certain handicaps. If she chooses (and many do), she can abort her child. Suppose there are two pregnant women who are both carrying children with the same handicap. One mother wants her baby; so the child lives. The other cannot imagine raising a child with special needs; so her baby is destroyed. Two children with exactly the same handicap, and one dies because of his or her parent's choice.

If we allow parents the absolute right over their newborn child's life, the same scenario could easily occur. Children with treatable handicaps would be sentenced to death at the whim of their parents, while others with the same condition would be allowed to live.

Children are not merely an extension of their parents.
While as Christians we uphold the authority and
strength of the family unit, we do not do so when parents prescribe death for their children. Not all parents
act in the best interest of their child, and when they fail
to do so, the law must intervene to protect the life of the
child.

Infanticide is a highly emotional issue in our society. Even for sincere people there is a tendency to say,
"But just this time, perhaps death would be best." We
often focus on a particular situation and think that it is
only one decision being made by one family. The infanticide advocates argue that it is a strictly private choice
between family and doctors. They tell us that it has no
bearing on society as a whole.

But that is just the point. *There are no purely private
decisions for death in our nation.* Every time a handicapped
child is denied medical treatment because someone says
his life is not worth living, all of our lives are affected.
The same laws that protect that child protect every one
of us. When we allow that protection to slip away from
just one child, it is really slipping away from all of us.

In the midst of muddled thinking and quality of life
judgments, we must clearly articulate principles of compassion and care for the handicapped infant. Killing is
never compassionate, and death is never the solution to a
difficult situation.

The Christian Alternative

While we work for the legal protection of the handicapped newborn, we must also realize that we fight this
evil on two fronts. It is not enough to say, "Save this
child." We must also be there to help the family care for
their special child. For example, the Christian Action
Council has begun a nationwide ministry to women with
crisis pregnancies. Any pregnant woman can come to
the center for counseling and practical help. Christian
counselors are trained to deal with a variety of difficult

pregnancy situations. Today hundreds of crisis pregnancy centers across the country are opening up to provide alternatives to abortion in the name of Jesus Christ.

Now we must apply this same type of love and Christian compassion to the family who is raising a handicapped child. Once again the needs are great and the situations are difficult—but not too difficult for those who know the power and love of Jesus Christ. Once again the Christian Action Council is initiating a program of care for the handicapped and elderly that will be directly sponsored by churches across the country. It will include respite care programs so that families who need a break will have a place to take their relatives. It will also include a day-care program sponsored by the church. Parent and family support groups are also planned, so families can find the emotional help they need within the local church.

What we are talking about here is churches becoming resource centers to the family in need. Along with this type of care, it is also time to begin specialized Sunday school classes for our mentally and physically handicapped. Even if no one in your own congregation has special needs, you can be sure there are many Christians in the community who do—and very few classes to meet those needs. The local church has a very important and often neglected part to play in this fight against infanticide.

For our family, this type of help is much more than a theory. In 1983, after years of involvement in the prolife movement, my husband Bill and I gave birth to our first child, Will. Will has Down's syndrome. Now we are learning, along with so many other parents, the joys and stresses of having a special child.

Having Will has certainly deepened our prolife convictions. When we look at his joyful personality, his love for life, and his abounding affection for friends and family, there is no doubt that he really is a special gift from God. His birth has brought home to us again the gruesome reality of abortion and infanticide in America. Many children like Will never make it out of the womb.

At the same time, raising Will has given us new insights into the special needs of parents and families of handicapped children. Although all of the parents of handicapped children we know dearly love their children, they may also find themselves faced with pain and difficulty most people never imagine. There is great joy in their lives, but also great stress and tension.

Families of handicapped children have special needs. The sad fact is that many of these needs go unmet when friends and neighbors who could do so much fail to act. Families break up, children do not receive proper care, and great emotional suffering occurs because Christians don't or won't step in to help.

Many of us think there is some kind of special training needed to work with handicapped citizens. In some cases this is true. But more often than not what is really needed is just some extra attention, love, and care to the simple needs around us.

Many more of us, whether we admit it to ourselves or not, are afraid of persons with a handicap. They are different than we are, and at first glance we can erect a wall between "normal" people and "abnormal" people that is difficult to break down. Often special children are not pretty to look at, and they respond differently than other children. Let's face it—there are many unpleasant and difficult situations involving handicapped children and their families. It is much easier to forget the whole mess and just go to prayer meeting. We just don't like to get our hands dirty.

But we do not have a choice. Unborn and newborn children are being killed in our country. As God's people, we know we must stand for their right to live. Yet, standing for life means much more than just being anti-abortion or anti-infanticide. It means we must help children and families with very practical needs. It means we must take the love and light of Jesus Christ into very dark situations. Let me share some practical ways that Christians can help on a personal basis.

Relieving the Stress
When a special child is born into a family, there is a stress created that never goes away. Parents must change their expectations and hopes for their child.

Teaching the child simple tasks can be a time-consuming and exhausting task. In some cases parents must face the fact that their child's condition will worsen. All of these factors come together to create extra tension in a family situation. All families experience difficulties and deal with a variety of tensions, but in a family with a special child there is a tension that never goes away. In the midst of career shifts, family deaths, and financial problems, there is the ever-present responsibility of a child who needs extra help.

Christians can help relieve that stress by offering to baby-sit on a regular basis or taking over family chores on a regular basis. These tasks sound so simple, but they can mean so much to a mother who is overwhelmed twenty-four hours a day with the care and feeding of her child. Parents need to be reminded that there really is life away from their child. They need the opportunity to relax and enjoy hobbies and activities that are completely unrelated to the care of their son or daughter.

Many children have complicated care rituals—special meals, extra equipment, or an intensive exercise program. Mothers and fathers need Christians within their church who are willing to make a commitment to help with these daily routines. Just knowing that someone else will be there in a few hours to help with lunchtime can be a busy mother's greatest help during the day.

These may seem like very small, practical steps to take to solve an overwhelming problem in our country.

Do not underestimate the difference just one caring person can make in the life of a child and family.

Recently I had an opportunity to participate in a workshop with another woman whose child was handicapped. Her little boy had been born several years ago with hydrocephalus, and his head was swollen from fluid that had gathered on his brain. Her boy had died last year, but God had given them three years together as a family before he took their child. It was wonderful to hear of the love and richness this boy had brought to his parents and brothers. She told the story of how one woman in the church had simply walked into her home one day and volunteered her help with the baby's care routine. Of course, like most new mothers, my friend was determined to do everything herself and was not about to entrust her baby to this woman. But this lady quietly persisted and kept in touch with my friend. Slowly but surely they became friends. It was just a few months later that my friend learned she had a tumor that had to be surgically removed. The surgery was complicated and the recovery a difficult one. She had to enter a special hospital hundreds of miles away. But because of the concern and care of this woman from her church, she knew her baby boy was in good hands.

It is just this kind of simple caring that makes the difference between life and death for a family. After all, there really are not that many handicapped children born in this country. Thankfully the majority of children are born healthy and remain that way throughout life. But for the small percentage who are born needing extra help, our personal efforts multiplied hundreds of times over can turn a tragic situation into one filled with hope and love.

Becoming a Resource
Education and information are real needs for families who suddenly find themselves with a special baby. Many times parents have never heard of their child's condition.

Many more times they have only vague ideas or horrible images of people they have known who had such handicaps. Very few people understand the many advances that have been made in caring for and understanding our citizens with a handicap. All over the country parent support groups have sprung up to help other parents deal with their child's handicap. Knowing you are not the only family to experience such a situation can bring enormous comfort. Early childhood intervention programs and specialized schooling opportunities give parents a variety of options from which to choose.

Christians can be a resource, providing parents with information and names, addresses, and telephone numbers of people who can help. The Rutherford Institute has compiled a list of organizations dedicated to providing help and information for special children and their families.* Many of them deal with a specific handicap, while others have been organized to provide legal rights and other opportunities for all of our citizens with handicaps.

Contact the Rutherford Institute for a copy of this list. Keep it handy, for someday you may find yourself in a position to provide important facts and resources for someone in your family, church, or neighborhood.

Helping
Infanticide is a problem that will not disappear. Even though Congress has now taken steps to protect handicapped newborn infants, we live in a country where human life is cheap. We abort one out of every three pregnancies in this country because having a baby just does not fit into our plans.

Can we really expect that this same attitude will not

---

* For a copy of this list, write or call: The Rutherford Institute, P. O. Box 510, Manassas, Virginia 22110; telephone: (703) 369-0100.

continue to spill over into our attitudes toward handicapped infants? Children are often no more than ornaments we choose to attach to our lives. If they are pretty ornaments, we keep them. However, many times it is much easier to just throw them away.

In the midst of this casual destruction of our most helpless human family members, we must continue to speak out for God's truth and his principles of love and care. Killing is never compassionate. Allowing a child to starve to death is never the most loving thing to do.

How do we fight infanticide in America? We speak out clearly for the care and equal protection of every citizen with a handicap. Every person is entitled to the full protection of our laws because every person shares equally in the image of God. No situation is so complex that the principles of providing care do not apply. Children are not merely an extension of their parents. No child can be denied acceptable medical treatment because someone thinks his or her life is not worth living.

In addition, we minister with Christian compassion to the child and family who has special needs. Within our churches and within our homes we must reach out to meet the needs around us. In the abortion issue, the response of the crisis pregnancy center ministry is proving that abortion is not the answer for anyone. We too must show the world that killing the child is never the answer.

Even though the handicapped child may not be perfect in the world's eyes, God has given him a unique gift and contribution to make. Our response is to help that person achieve his or her potential and to show our society that what may be a tragedy in the world's eyes can be a glorious success in the eyes of God.

5
LIGHT House
by Marilyn Lewis

On January 31, 1984, in Washington, D.C. at the National Religious Broadcasters Convention, Franky Schaeffer delivered what turned out for us to be a life-changing message. He was speaking in place of his father and using his father's text, but the urgency in Franky's voice and spirit made us want to act. There were sixteen people from our staff in Washington. That night we went back to our hotel suite and talked into the night. We had been stirred! We had to do something! Our conversation ran mainly along the lines of how we could use our ministry with young people (Kansas City Youth for Christ) to make teenagers aware of the issues.

The next day, however, Jerry Falwell spoke at a luncheon and told of the Save-A-Baby ministry. This clicked in our minds and hearts. We had come to Washington on a big over-the-road bus, and all the way home we brainstormed about what we could do in Kansas City. In the middle of the night, somewhere between Kansas City and Washington, D.C., our staff held hands and covenanted together with the Lord that we would start a ministry to help girls with problem pregnancies. Our dream was big, but not as big as it was to become!

The first instruction I received was that our staff was so overloaded that if this was to become a reality, the Lord would have to provide new help. Being a volunteer—the wife of a TV station general manager—I could pick my hours and my job. This is what I believed the Lord would have me do.

The Property

I set out to look for property. At times I got discouraged. I thought it was never going to really happen! Then I thought I found the "perfect" property. It was bursting with charm, it would handle fifty girls, and it just needed a "little" renovating.

When I rounded up the top ten men of our organization to go see it, they declared that all this property needed was a case of dynamite! Well, on to Plan B, C, D, etc. I asked my father if he thought it was ever going to happen and he said, "As soon as you find that perfect property, everything will gel at once."

Around the first of September, a Catholic man who watched our TV station heard us talking about our dream. He called me and said, "I have just the place." He told me about a thirty-five-year-old convent in Kansas City that was for sale. I knew the place! It was a Kansas City landmark, an architectural beauty that students from the art institute studied.

This gentleman arranged for us to meet the Catholic Sisters and see the convent. The minute we walked in, we knew this was the place for us. It even had a sitz bath and infirmary. It was perfect in every way, except the price.

The question immediately arose: How big was my faith? To replace a ninety-four thousand square foot building of this quality on six prime acres in the heart of one of the most beautiful areas of Kansas City would cost ten million dollars. We had nothing. However, we would be able to handle between one hundred to one hundred and fifty girls in these facilities, which would mean saving three hundred to four hundred and fifty babies per year!

We came to the negotiating table with six Catholic

Sisters, prayed together, and then set out to tell them where our heart was. We knew that there were other organizations wanting to purchase the same beautiful piece of property who were planning to offer more money than we felt we could. Originally I had felt that we could never possibly raise more than $500,000 to purchase and equip this type of facility. I had to come to the place in my own heart where I said, "Lord, this is your work, and if we have to pay this much for this property, then I will trust you to provide."

We finally agreed on a price of $750,000 to be paid in cash (we always operate on a cash basis) by December 31. The date was October 7, and we had no money! Besides that, we needed to raise a total of $1,200,000 in order to bring it up to code and equip it for occupancy.

The miraculous thing is that the other potential buyers were offering cash—and more of it. The Sisters knew that we had *no* money, and yet they agreed to sell to us because they liked the cause. We offered them a $20,000 check for earnest money. However, they gave it back to us and said, "We know you are serious. Your word is better than your money!"

Next, we went on a fact-finding trip with a Christian attorney, doctor, pilot, and three staff members to Lynchburg, Virginia and Birmingham, Alabama. We learned that no one else was doing anything of this magnitude. Were we dreaming too big?

Jerry Falwell assured us that we were doing what must be done in every major city. The people at Save-A-Baby ministry told us that they could fill our place to capacity tomorrow! This was our confirmation from the Lord.

An Awareness Blitz

Because of the short amount of time before December 31, we put our heads together and started planning by faith that the Sisters would accept our proposal. In a one-day brainstorming session with six people on our staff, we named the home and planned the strategy for raising the funds.

The name, we believe, was inspired by the Lord. It was LIGHT House.

LIGHT stands for Life Is Given Hope for Tomorrow. Besides that, the place looks like a lighthouse. It stands on a hill with a six-story bell tower that houses four tremendous bells. You can hear those bells all over the countryside, and we are going to ring those bells every time we save a baby! The Sisters at the convent said that they rang them when someone died, and I think they liked our idea better!

How to raise the money? We decided that the first thing we had to do was to organize a LIGHT House Action Committee. Of course, the Lord chose to use mostly women for this. We got on the phone and called the most prolife, active, involved women we could think of in the Kansas City area (you know, the ones who do everything and whose calendars are already booked), and invited them to a meeting in three days at my house to let them know what was happening. Seventy women showed up that day. As I stood before them and told them that at that very moment the Sisters were signing the purchase agreement with our executive director, Al Metsker, and our lawyer, the room was filled with tears and gratefulness. Finally there was something *positive* to do in the prolife movement!

We outlined our strategy for raising the funds—which was so new that there were really no details—and then asked for people to volunteer in their or their husband's field of expertise. Because of the caliber of women we were working with, a tremendous groundwork was laid that day.

We explained that our first big push had to be an awareness blitz. We wanted press from every form of media and speaking engagements in every church and service organization that would have us. Some volunteered to write news releases and send them everywhere. Others said that their husbands were heads of organizations, and they would contact those groups. Some volunteered their artistic talents, and we enlisted some of them as public speakers. We decided that we would print up postage-paid envelopes that explained our project and try to get businesses, utility companies, and banks to include them in their statements, and some of the women volunteered to work on that.

We felt that this whole project—if it actually became a reality—would only happen because of the supernatural power of God. We appointed a prayer chairman to head up the prayer groups around the city. It soon became apparent that we were going about this backwards if we did not include the pastors on the ground floor. Thus, we planned a pastors' luncheon. We put on another phone blitz, inviting every pastor we could contact, and about one hundred pastors came for lunch and to hear about the LIGHT House. The pastors were excited, pledged their support, and signed up for bulletin inserts and guest speakers to come to their church.

Because the first Monday women's meeting had been so "spur of the moment" and there were some that had not come, we planned a second meeting for the next Monday. About one hundred more women came and caught the vision. During this week-long interval between Monday meetings, the Lord brought several confirming miracles to mind.

● A local businessman watched Jerry Falwell on TV on a Sunday morning as he told about the Save-A-Baby ministry. Something clicked and he told his wife, "We are going to purchase the Benedictine convent and turn it into a Save-A-Baby Home." He called his daughter, who was a nurse (RN) at a local hospital, and told her that she was going to run it. Then he called the convent to tell the Sisters. They informed him that the Sisters had agreed the day before on a price with Kansas City Youth for Christ to be used for just that purpose. So this businessman got involved with our fund-raising project.

• A local artist called and asked what she could do to help. We said we needed a logo yesterday. In less than twenty-four hours she was at our office with five different logos to pick from—all of them beautiful. We picked one, and twenty-four hours later it was being printed on our material! Our print shop worked around the clock to print materials for handouts explaining how to promote the LIGHT House.

• A top executive from an international firm came to our Monday meeting and said that the Lord had laid on her heart to write a proposal to go after corporate and foundation money. She began working to draw up that time-consuming document. A CPA called the same day and said he would be delighted to do the research and to produce a yearly budget, which is required in these proposals.

• Another woman, whose husband is one of the best graphic artists in the city, volunteered his services to design brochures and the telethon set.

• Hospitals started calling, wanting to get in on the action and deliver our babies. We are currently negotiating with them for the best package deal.

• Medical doctors, registered nurses, pharmacists, technicians, child-birth instructors, etc. began calling and offering their services.

• A young Christian attorney vowed to see this thing through to the end and for no charge has assisted in every negotiation that might have legal implications. He is securing our licensing as a home for minors and an adoption agency. His unselfishness has been a tremendous testimony.

• A woman who has had thirty-two years experience in the teaching profession, beginning with all eight grades in a one-room school and expanding to advisory and administrative positions, called to say that she wanted to serve the Lord. Her call came at a time when the LIGHT House had just been born, and she had not heard about it. She became our director.

• Another woman got wind of the LIGHT House. Her expertise is in the field of adoption, with fifteen years experience working with judges. She came to work for us. It gave us instant credibility with the social services and the adoption judges.

• Our entire staff caught the vision and doubled their load. Volunteers came from everywhere to "pitch in," working full workloads without any pay.

• The Neighborhood Association where the convent is located called and asked us to come and explain to them exactly what we have in mind for this property. The Association explained that it could "make or break" us with zoning permits. We went to see them and just laid it all out before them. When we were done, they were so excited that they wanted us to bring them some sponsor sheets so they could help us raise funds in the Walk-A-Thon.

• I went to a prolife banquet to tell my story. Afterwards a man came up to me and said he was a member of the architectural firm that drew up the plans for the convent. He said he had the scale model in his attic and asked if we wanted it. He brought it over, and the Lord has used that scale model tremendously to demonstrate the magnitude of the building and the beauty of the architecture in raising funds. It has helped people catch the vision for our work.

• An executive from the Motherhood Maternity Shop called me and asked if we wanted some brand-new maternity clothes. Of course I said yes. Her reply was,

"Send me two volunteers to cut out labels, and make sure you bring a truck." We received $12,000 worth of new maternity clothes to begin our home with!

● Another man and his wife told me with tears that they felt the Lord leading them to deliver the message of the LIGHT House to churches in the outlying areas. He had an idea for a film presentation and script. I appreciated their spirit and willingness, but had no way to produce the slide presentation. The next day a professional photographer came to see me and said, "Act as though you have hired me. Tell me what to do, but I will not send you a bill." I got him in touch with the man writing the script, and they are making it a reality.

● We got word that Franky Schaeffer was planning to be in our town for some TV taping. We called him and said, "Hey, you got us into this. Will you do a special kickoff rally for us?" He was delighted!

Why Us?

The reason we became involved in a project like this in the first place is because God led us to do it. But as we reflect, we feel there are probably three main reasons why the Lord is using our organization so mightily.

(1) We are interdenominational. This is a cause that crosses all the political, denominational, and racial barriers. It is easier for everyone to become involved when it is an interdenominational organization or multichurch group that is spearheading it.

(2) We are credible. Kansas City Youth for Christ has been around for forty-two years, and we have the reputation for doing what we say we are going to do. We currently own two teen ranches, a sixteen hundred-seat auditorium, and office facilities. These facilities are totally paid for. We have a "cash" policy which never allows us to borrow money.

(3) We also have a TV station. When we decide to

do something, we run up to the tech center and make some spots, plan specials, or preempt regular programming.

Franky Schaeffer Rally

When we got word that Franky Schaeffer would be willing to help us in our kickoff rally, and that we actually had a convent to buy, we had two weeks to put it together. We promoted the event on television spots and also planned to air it live that night. To round out the evening, we had our staff arranger and musician put together a really "big" song with brass and teenage music groups on the LIGHT House. We changed some of the words to fit the occasion. This song has become our theme song. I addressed the audience and told about the LIGHT House concept, our first "official" announcement, and then we put Franky on to speak. Franky volunteered to promote the Walk-A-Thon while he spoke. He gave a stirring hour-long speech. When he was done, we opened up the phone lines for people to ask questions and offer money. The phones went crazy—eighteen lines! When the evening was over, we had raised over $18,000, and 152 people had signed up to walk in the Walk-A-Thon. We were on the way!

Walk-A-Thon

Plans for the Walk-A-Thon started to gel. The original motivation for having a Walk-A-Thon was to give teenagers the opportunity to become involved. We had lived up to the commitment that we had made in Washington, D.C.—to make teenagers aware of the issues—and now they wanted to do something. We would walk ten miles on a Saturday. We would originate the walk at the YFC headquarters, walk five miles (the most scenic route in Kansas City) to the convent, have lunch there, take a tour of the facilities, and then walk back five miles. We would climax the day with a gigantic victory rally.

Originally we hoped that we could have fifteen hundred walkers and raise a quarter of a million dollars. We would use the money to kick off our telethon, which we hoped would bring in the balance. As time progressed, however, we went past the two thousand mark. The day before the walk, we had thirty-three hundred people signed up to walk.

When I woke up on Saturday morning, the day of the Walk-A-Thon, I looked out of my window to see blizzard conditions. The temperature was in the thirties, and wet snow was blowing wildly. I bundled up and went to the headquarters.

Even though it was an hour and half before the walk, there was traffic everywhere. The walkers were going to do it anyway! The police came to try to direct traffic, but finally threw up their hands and left. Walkers carried babies, pushed strollers and buggies, and carried banners. We wanted this to be a real media event. Each walker had a red helium-filled balloon pinned to his shoulder. The sight was tremendous.

Businesses donated groceries for the lunch. Churches along the route donated their bathroom facilities. Scores of people donated their administrative assistance. We had live music set up outside the convent and a huge charcoal grill. Everyone ate sloppy joes and hot dogs.

The entire time that these people were walking, volunteers at the headquarters were trying to tabulate the amounts pledged. The statistics were amazing. There were a total of 3,309 people that walked, and they raised a total of $432,000!

The youngest person to go on the walk was a two-month-old baby; the oldest was an eighty-four-year-old woman. A man with an artificial foot made the entire walk, as did two blind people and one person in a wheelchair.

The three major secular TV stations covered the

walk on their two evening newscasts. The people they interviewed, though freezing to the bone, exclaimed that they were glad to walk in bad weather because it demonstrates how serious they are about this issue. This is not just a fair-weather issue; it is a matter of life and death!

Telethon

We figured that the total amount of money that we would have to raise in order to prepare the LIGHT House for opening would be $1,200,000. We wanted to have that all pledged by the end of the telethon.

The eight-day telethon began the day after the Walk-A-Thon and lasted for eight days. We started the numbers on our tally board at $475,000 (the $432,000 that was pledged on the Walk-A-Thon plus another $43,000 that had come in previously). From previous telethons we had calculated how much we must accomplish during each of the eight days. We were on target every day except one.

For two weeks prior to the telethon we had aired spots asking people to donate handcrafted items, antiques, and new merchandise to be used as appreciation gifts during the telethon. People started bringing in afghans, quilts, furs, valuable glass, furniture, and antiques. We were inundated with merchandise.

We also asked people to donate large amounts of money that we could use as "challenge money," and the people responded. Challenges went like this: we would put a timer on the TV screen, set it for a certain amount of time, and someone would agree to donate $1,000 if others would call in and pledge another thousand dollars in smaller amounts in the specified amount of time. It made a real exciting game out of fund-raising. The telethon was filled with testimonies from adopted children, women who have had abortions, parents of unwed mothers, and so on.

As the week went along, we often ran out of challenge money. Thus, we would tell the viewers that we were out. The Lord always provided someone else to call in with more thousands.

We also ran out of appreciation gifts; so we put out a plea for more merchandise. People responded by bringing in sentimental gifts and valuable items. When questioned about it, they always replied that nothing material is as valuable as one human life. One eight-year-old boy heard that we needed more appreciation gifts; so he told his mother that he wanted to give his hand-painted Pennsylvania rocker. His mother wisely agreed to it. When he brought it over to the station, he went on television and said that he wanted it to be used to save babies. Someone pledged $1,000 for it! What a great lesson in giving that little boy learned. A pastor's wife donated her mink stole, and we offered it as an appreciation gift for $3,000. Someone else pledged the $3,000 and gave it back to the pastor's wife. One of the thrills of the week was to see how many teenagers and children pledged. These kids already know where they stand on the prolife issue!

The week was full of heart-rending stories of sacrifice, blessing, and miracles. Our total board was on the front of a huge jack-in-the-box. Every time we had a new total we would crank the handle and out would pop a clown who bent over and changed the total. We also had a tremendous grandstand which started out the week with four hundred and seventy-five baby dolls, representing the first $475,000 that had been raised. Every time we raised another thousand, we would add another baby until the grandstand would be full with twelve hundred babies!

We called Jerry Falwell and asked him if he could drop by the telethon during his travels across the country. He called back and said he could give us one hour on Monday afternoon. During the hour that he was there (which was also a holiday, so people were home), we raised $19,000. Momentum was growing!

Our last night was Sunday night November 18. We were scheduled to quit at midnight.

We started the telethon day on Sunday with $1,031,140. We had to raise $169,000 that day to make it. Miracles started to happen.

Churches started calling in and saying that they were giving us their evening offering or a thousand dollars out of their missionary budget. Pastors came over to endorse the project, and people in general really caught the vision.

By 9:30 P.M. it was obvious that the end was near. Excitement was building. At 9:45—ahead of schedule—we hit the $1,200,000 mark. Pandemonium broke loose. We celebrated for one hour. Then we declared that we would open the phone lines until midnight—the official end of the telethon—for people to call in monthly pledges. All of the twenty-four lines lit up again. When midnight came, the total raised toward the purchase of the building was $1,224,151 and $2,860 in monthly pledges.

The day after the telethon, people were still calling in to pledge, offer assistance, or give us goods and services. For example, one man who works with an X-ray company called to say that his company wanted to give us a Sonogram machine.

Two days after the telethon, we were scheduled to come up for a zone change before the zoning board. When we stood to start presenting our case, the official stopped us and asked, "Wait—is this the organization that just raised all the money?" We said, "Yes." He said, "There's nothing more to discuss. I approve."

How the Facilities Will Be Used

Girls who will be invited to stay at the LIGHT House will be those that are considered "abortion risks"—that is, they have either had a previous abortion or have one already scheduled. When they come to our facilities, we will be meeting them at one of the lowest points of their lives.

Our first objective will be to help them in their spiritual life. We want to teach each girl to have a meaningful walk with the Lord. After that, our goal is to help the girl continue her education and to teach her a trade in order to keep her off the welfare rolls.

We are going to do this in several ways. First, if a girl has not graduated from high school, we will offer her the opportunity to be placed in a GED program. Otherwise, we will tailor a curriculum to maintain her grade level while she is out of school.

Each girl will be required to learn to type, because this opens a broad range of job possibilities. We are purchasing IBM Selectric II typewriters for this purpose. Girls will also be taught sewing, essentials of proper nutrition, and child development and care.

For the vocational training, we will be running a business, and our facilities lend themselves perfectly for this. Our business will include a restaurant, and the girls will learn that you have to take in more money than you pay out. They will also learn how to cook, serve, and maintain quality control. Along with the restaurant, we will operate a boutique, in which we will sell the many hand-crafted items and ceramics that the girls make. Consider what has already happened in terms of our vo-tech program.

• One lady called to say that she had a lucrative candy business that operated out of her home. She wanted to come and teach the girls the fun of candy-making and have a candy store in the boutique.

• A beautician offered to train the girls to wear makeup properly and promised to cut all the girls' hair.

• A businessman offered to keep us supplied with shampoo, rinse, lotion, and other like items.

• A man and his wife, who own a ceramic shop,

told us that they had a kiln, three thousand to four thousand molds, three glass display cases, shelving, and work tables. They told us they wanted to give the whole shop to the LIGHT House for the girls to learn ceramics and make items to sell in the boutique.

● Another lady called and said that a full-service quilt-making supplier had closed down. She thought it would be wonderful to help the girls sponsor a corner of our boutique for quilting supplies. She also wanted to teach the girls the art of making quilts.

● A manicurist teacher volunteered to teach the girls to become manicurists, with no charge for tuition.

● A graphic artist volunteered to teach the girls the basics of paste-up. This is a field where there is always a demand.

● Soon after the Franky Schaeffer kickoff rally, a young couple called and said they were interested in helping with the restaurant at the LIGHT House. When I questioned them further, I learned that they both were currently managing four of the best restaurants in Kansas City. They had a degree in hotel and restaurant management. They had wanted to be missionaries, and they felt that this was their calling. They wanted to devote their lives to this project.

Our objective is to teach the girls trades they can do at home so they can still be mothers to their babies and *not* be on the welfare rolls. Other fields they will be learning are flower arranging, drapery making, upholstering, data processing, and more to come. We will offer not only an alternative to abortion, but an alternative to welfare.

The LIGHT House's beautiful six acres already have fruit trees and grapevines, but next summer the world will witness the best organic garden in the Midwest. The girls will become gardeners!

The chapel, which seats five hundred, is going to become an interdenominational prayer headquarters for

Kansas City. The chapel will be dedicated to the memory of the unborn dead and will open to the public for prayer. We want people to come here and pray for America and pray for ways to save unborn children.

Churches have already inquired about renting the chapel. Individuals may also rent the chapel, which has a pipe organ for weddings and other events. This will also provide added income. Nationally known entertainers have also volunteered to come and do black-tie concerts in the chapel.

How Will We Finance It?

Financing will come from several sources. The biggest source of income will be God's people who give sacrificially because they feel this is one of the greatest stop-gaps available in the abortion issue.

Another source of income will be adoptive parents. (Statistics tell us that half of the girls, once they have decided against abortion, will adopt out their babies.) The restaurant, boutique, and vo-tech end of the LIGHT House will produce some income, as will the rental of the chapel.

What's in the Future?

Currently we are busy preparing the facilities so we can move in. We have hired some of our key personnel and still have more to pick. Girls are already calling us—needing a place to go.

The urgency is ever before us. We must hurry! There are over four thousand babies being killed every day.

Never in all of my life have I seen such a unifying project! I had one man come up to me and offer to help on the LIGHT House. He told me not to discuss any other issue with him because we probably would not agree. However, he said that he wanted to help us make this a reality.

Every denomination has joined in enthusiastically.

Even those who are prochoice are admitting that this is truly a viable "choice" and are sharing our vision. Virtually every prolife group has jumped into this project with both feet, with no thought of who might get the credit. We all simply want the job to get done.

During the entire telethon, we received reports from around the country that we were being watched. We told our television audience that they carried an awesome responsibility because we were not only going to save babies in Kansas City, but were also setting the pace for the nation.

Others in major cities were watching to see if it could really be done. If we did it, maybe they could too. Consequently, we were not only saving three hundred babies per year in our facilities, but hopefully thousands of babies.

Our hope is that *you* will decide to do this in *your* town. It is a matter of life and death, and the Lord is looking for someone who will say, "Use me." The rewards are tremendous. The satisfaction is beyond description.

6
Sidewalk Counseling and Picketing
by Joseph M. Scheidler

Many people believe the prolife movement is a national organization, with its headquarters in Washington, D.C. They think it must have national leaders whom all prolifers look up to and take their orders from. But the prolife movement does not. It is a grass-roots movement that puts the heat on from the bottom up. We may not be able to reverse *Roe v. Wade* overnight. However, we *can* close down the abortion industry in our cities and neighborhoods.

The battles have to be fought on the battlefields, and the abortion battlefields are everywhere. So prolife people have to be organized on the *local* level to fight these *local* battles.

What effective leaders should do is organize effective local programs and find the leadership in the area where these programs are needed. Next, they should stay in touch with that leadership and encourage the local troops to do the work that has to be done where they are.

The successful prolife movement is little cells of prolife activists all over the country, closing down the clinics in their locales and offering alternatives to women. This keeps abortions out of your own town or neighborhood. It requires setting up pregnancy-help agencies, educating local high school students, parents, and teachers, and getting into the classrooms to use a basic, simple story—that *every* life is precious and that abortion is murder.

The American citizen is a person of tremendous power and importance. We should recognize this quality and use it. That is why it is so exciting to see the prolife movement expressing the will of the people.

The prolife movement can be successful in the hands of the people because the power structure in this country is based on "we the people." If the people do not want something, they will generally work successfully against it. If they do not like the system the way it is and the things that are decided for them, they will eventually change it. That is really what America is all about.

The American people, with some local exceptions, were never allowed to vote on abortion. Abortion on demand was handed to Americans by a Supreme Court fiat through a deliberate proabortion misinterpretation of the Constitution. Nevertheless, Americans *can* stop abortion if they are willing to make sacrifices of time and commitment.

Citizen Power
The power of the individual to change history is never exercised more strikingly than when a person goes to an abortion clinic, confronts a woman who is going in, talks her out of having an abortion, and so preserves the life of a human child. That is something each of us *can* do as an individual.

We *can* save a life. In doing so, we perpetuate decency, morality, righteousness, the spirit of the Constitution, and the spirit of the law.

We can have an on-the-spot reversal of the *Roe v Wade* and the *Doe v Bolton* abortion decisions on a one-to-one basis at the doorstep of the abortion clinic. It can be done. There are prolife sidewalk counselors who have stopped fifteen or twenty abortions in one day in just one place!

If a few can do it, it would seem that every Christian who wanted to could also do it. This shows the power of the individual and the strength of our arguments. It proves that life is stronger than death and is a powerful weapon against all enemies—the courts, the media, feminist propaganda, and powerful groups like the American Medical Association. It says that the dedicated prolife activist can defeat the enemy through his ability to convince and persuade. It is a lifesaving use of his constitutional right of free speech.

Thus, *whenever you talk about the prolife movement, you are in fact talking about yourself.* The movement is powerful because it consists of individuals working hand-in-hand with the best traditions of this country (those still based on the Judeo-Christian ethic).

If we do our job, the collapse of the abortion industry in America is only a matter of time. The question is, do we really want to stop abortion now?

Sidewalk Counseling

Sidewalk counseling is probably the single most valuable activity that a prolife person can do. During the time prolifers are counseling in front of an abortion clinic, they are coming between the woman and the abortionist, between the baby who is scheduled to be killed and the abortionist who is planning to kill him or her.

There is no one way to do sidewalk counseling. The counselor has to know something about human nature and about psychology. He must be able to try and understand the crisis the woman is facing. The counselor has to understand what has driven her to this unnatural, barbaric solution to a "problem" pregnancy—the decision to kill her baby. The worst solution to any human problem is to kill an innocent human being. Yet, that is the solution she has chosen. Something drove her to that. Some people may think it is such a horrendous decision that once it is made there is no way to turn the woman back. But she can be turned back.

For example, *in Chicago, in one thirty-day period, half*

a dozen sidewalk counselors were able to stop ninety women from having abortions. Seventeen were stopped in a single morning at a single clinic. While a few of these women may have had their abortions later, more than 90 percent did not. Moreover, they kept in touch with the counseling center. Sidewalk counselors were present to intercept them at the clinic. Someone cared that their babies lived.

An example I use sometimes to bring home the reality of abortion is to ask: If someone came into your home and grabbed your three-year-old, rushed out of the house, threw the child into an automobile, and drove off, what would you do? Would you write a letter to the newspaper editor? Would you complain to your congressman? Would you ask the police to give better protection to your neighborhood? No, you wouldn't do any of those things. You would rush out of the house, jump in your car, and pursue that kidnapper in order to save your child's life. If you saw the kidnapper taking your child into a building, you would go into that building. No one could keep you out. You would go where the child is in danger. You would try to save him. This is what we are doing when we go to an abortion clinic.

What to Do
The counselor can approach gently and ask the woman if she wants to talk. Some counselors will take "no" for an answer and not pursue. Others will refuse to take "no" and will try various techniques. Some people try to win the woman over by a cheerful greeting. Next, they offer her literature, something not repugnant to her, such as a picture of a baby or a pregnant woman.

Other counselors will simply get down to brass tacks and say, "Have you thought about the baby? Have you thought about what abortion does? Have you thought about your own health, your own body?" Counselors who have been doing this for years do not become discouraged by rejection. Most attempts do end in rejection. In fact, at least nine out of ten women approached will go on into the abortion clinic. We are often called uncomplimentary names. People strike out at prolife counselors and brush them aside. *But whatever the reaction, the attempt is positive and is possibly the only effort that has been made to save the baby's life.* A peaceful presence and a positive approach to this serious problem can be most effective.

One method that has been found to be very effective in dissuading women from abortions is to inform them of the malpractice suits against the clinic because of the damage done to women there. As we get to know more and more women who have been to a particular abortion clinic and have suffered physical and psychological trauma as a result of their abortions, we can approach other women with an example from an actual malpractice court case. One Chicago clinic, considered to be one of the "best in town," has twenty-two outstanding malpractice suits against it. We have been outside the clinic on at least three occasions when an ambulance has pulled up to take away an injured woman who went there for an abortion.

To find out about malpractice suits, go to the courthouse and study cases coming up for hearings. The charges, the doctors' names, the clinic's name, and the dates—all of these and many more facts are available to the public.

We have discovered that sometimes the woman, especially if she is young, does not realize that the life inside of her is as well developed as it is at her stage of gestation. The clinic personnel have told her that it is not even a baby yet—that it's only tissue. They have lied to her to get her to have the abortion. Unlike prolife activists, they are not there out of concern for anyone, but only to make money.

Once counselors talk to the woman about fetal development and show her pictures of what her baby looks like and how well developed the baby is, she may change her mind. Sometimes all it takes is to have someone there with the facts of fetal development and the facts of abortion. The woman is not going to get any facts inside the clinic. The only "choice" the clinic wants her to make is not an informed one, but one for abortion.

If a woman is willing to talk, it is extremely helpful if there is a pregnancy crisis center to refer her to or take her to. Prolife citizens are trying to set up pregnancy crisis centers near every abortion clinic. At these centers women can get a pregnancy test and talk with a counselor. In Chicago, most abortions are stopped at clinics where there is such a center nearby—where women can get immediate help.

It is not enough to give a woman a phone number and tell her to call in a few days. The more immediate the alternative is, the better chance there is of stopping the abortion. (Why is it that so few churches have a crisis pregnancy center? Often churches are *very near* abortion clinics, but have not even bothered to find out, let alone help.)

It will be necessary for the counselor to follow through, get the woman's phone number and first name, and continue to help her through the pregnancy. It is not enough to talk a woman out of an abortion. The counselor must follow up to make sure she does not waver in her decision to carry the baby to term. A counselor may have to help in other ways, such as by getting a doctor, finding a place for her to stay, getting her medical help. Whatever problem is making her decide on an abortion is going to have to be solved. Perhaps it is a matter of talking to the parents or husband or boyfriend. The counselor, with the help of a crisis pregnancy center, must help make this as livable a decision as possible.

People are always asking me if I have professional counselors and I say, "No, not if we can help it." I have heard too many complaints about professional counselors. Dozens of people have told me they've gotten very little help, if any, from the counselors they have gone to—professional counselors who charge $50 an hour. I am certain there are good professional counselors around, but it is not essential to have them for our work.

In counseling, remember that if you have true concern and compassion for both victims of abortion—the mother as well as the baby—you are better qualified to talk to women going into a clinic to have an abortion than the "counselors" inside the clinic. In most cases, such "counselors" have received no special training that gives them an advantage over you. Any "counselor" who would recommend that a client kill her unborn baby and run the risk of physical damage associated with abortion is unqualified to counsel.

Before counseling at the abortion clinic nearest you, make a visit to the place to study the geographic set-up. You need to know if the public has access to the building the clinic is in or whether it is a private development. How close can you get to the entrance through which clinic customers will walk? You want to come into personal contact with these women if at all possible. However, if there is a private parking lot or walkway preventing this, your strategy will have to take this into consideration.

If you have any doubts at all about what is private and what is public, you can find out easily enough by walking up to the entrance or onto the parking lot to talk to women going in. You will soon find out! If you are breaking the law, clinic personnel will call the police and they, in turn, will show you where you're allowed to walk and where you cannot. It is that simple (although you cannot always trust the police to take your full rights as citizens into consideration). If what they tell you seems unreasonably restrictive, go to city hall or the town's municipal building and look up the ordinances. Unless there are warnings already posted—such as "no trespassing," "customers only," "patients only"—you will probably not be arrested unless you refuse to obey police orders to leave or move further away.

Regardless of whether the clinic is on public or private property, go inside and ask about the services they provide. Do not be afraid. They will not know who you are or what you are doing there the first time. While there, you can see what kind of counseling is provided and get familiar with the layout of the place and the kind of people working there.

In talking to the pregnant women who approach the clinic, you want them, above all, to stop and talk to you and take the literature you have to offer them. Be sure to talk to them one on one. Several people speaking or trying to counsel one woman can be threatening and distracting. It is good to have another counselor nearby in case help is needed, but one counselor alone should do the counseling.

Approach the women in a friendly manner and know exactly what you are going to say. You do not have much time—often only seconds—to convince them that you are genuinely interested and concerned and that you can help them out—that you have something positive and helpful to offer, *a real alternative.*

Try something like, "Hello. My name is Mary. I have some literature to offer you. Please take it. I'm here to offer women alternatives to abortion. Are you coming here for an abortion? A pregnancy test? Do you know someone who is?"

If some of the women you approach seem hostile, don't even mention abortion. Have a copy of *Body Ecology* or the *Clinic Check List* handy and tell them it has useful information about their reproductive health, important facts they ought to have but will not receive in the clinic. Of course, you must be very familiar with all the literature you pass out, so that you can call some particular

fact to their attention, something that will help to pro-
long the conversation, or so you can answer any question
that might be asked.

Once you have the woman's attention, you want to
keep it at all costs. Thus, do not stop talking to her and
keep trying to get her to talk. Ask her questions. Ask her
what her religion is, if she's married or single, if she has
any other children, if her doctor sent her here, if she has
ever met or spoken to the doctor who is about to operate
on her. Ask anything to get her talking about herself.
Offer to buy her a cup of coffee or a Coke.

A woman getting an abortion is required *not* to eat
before the operation. Thus, once she has sat down with
you over a cup of coffee and a sweet roll she is much less
likely to break off the conversation and proceed with her
plans.

Invite her to a nearby restaurant or coffee shop—
anything to get her (and her baby) away from the clinic
and into surroundings more conducive to calm, confi-
dential counseling. Once she has agreed to sit down and
talk with you, you have virtually stopped an abortion.
This is because there should be no help she needs that
you cannot provide, from convincing information about
the humanity and development of her unborn child, to
medical, legal, or marital problems.

Stay in Touch
If you succeed in talking a woman out of an abortion,
keep in touch with her faithfully. Offer her your home
address and telephone number. Tell her she can call
collect if necessary. Ask her how you can reach her with
help. Try to get her phone number or some address
where she can be reached for follow-up, while promising
to respect her privacy.

A woman who has been pressured into an abortion
may still have to face that pressure when she decides

against it. She may decide to return to the clinic if she doubts that you are willing and able to help her as you promised.

Remember, you cannot talk a woman out of an abortion and leave her to face her problems by herself. You have a certain obligation to her. Thus, call her back sometime that same day or evening and offer to bring her baby clothes or make whatever arrangements are necessary to meet her needs. This may be an inconvenience and place additional financial burdens on you, but that goes with the job.

Of course, it's essential to make arrangements with doctors, hospitals, and agencies beforehand. Be sure to have addresses and phone numbers of those who can and will assist. Do not just give the woman their names. Offer to take her there to make sure she gets what she needs when she needs it. This means, in short, that *you* must be available.

The Picket and Demonstration
The peaceful demonstration or picket is one of the most effective tools prolifers have to stop abortions and to eventually *close down abortion clinics*. During one year in Chicago a senior citizen picketed a single abortion clinic every day—despite rain, heat, or freezing temperature—and literally closed the clinic. Despite jeers from many passersby, as well as threats by clinic owners and attorneys, he continued passing out literature, talking to clients, and carrying a picket sign presenting the value of unborn human life. He remained at his post until the clinic closed a few days before he died.

Even more effective than the small picket is the massive demonstration in front of a clinic that makes entering the clinic difficult. Many potential clients do not want to pass through a moving picket line or risk being photographed if the media are present (which is more likely when the crowd is large).

Pickets must be well planned, well organized, and orderly. Signs should be carefully checked before being used. Anything crude, insulting, or off the subject should be rejected. Wording on picket signs should be large, concise, uncomplicated, and to the point.

Abortionists want the money they make from abortions, not the credit for doing them. Do everything possible to expose who is doing the abortions in your community. Names of clinic owners, operators, and doctors may be used on the signs. ABORTION KILLS BABIES. ABORTION IS MURDER. DON'T ABORT YOUR BABY. GIVE LIFE A CHANCE. LIFE YES—ABORTION NO. ADOPTION YES—ABORTION NO. These are examples of slogans that come to the point and zero in on the subject and the attitude. Lengthy quotes may be effective if photographed for a newspaper or magazine article where they can be read in full (though these are generally unclear for television). Large, single-subject photographs of live babies or aborted babies are useful, but small cutout pictures do not work well.

Every picket should have marshals appointed who indicate the parameters, keep the picket moving, watch spacing, prevent bunching-up, and in general maintain order and discipline. Marshals should wear some distinctive badge or armband.

Name-calling or any acts that may give a bad image to the picket or to the prolife movement must be discouraged. Carrying signs, praying, chanting information slogans, and singing are proper activities during the picket.

The marshal who gives direction and leads vocal action should have a megaphone or bullhorn. He should welcome suggestions from the group, but should not allow conflicting messages, songs, or slogans to be called out simultaneously. Generally, simple slogans, songs, and prayers, led alternately, will occupy the group, with occasional periods of complete silence. It is impressive to see a crowd of a hundred or more pickets walking in complete silence before an abortion clinic.

A picket on a public sidewalk is advised to keep moving, generally single file in a long oval. It should move slowly enough so that children, adults carrying children or pushing babies, and elderly members do not tire. Demonstrations, especially if arrangements have been made for speakers, do not have to keep moving.

During the picket the sidewalk must not be blocked, and entrances and exits must maintain free access. Otherwise there will be problems with the police.

Police should be notified of the picket in advance. When they arrive, a representative of the group should introduce himself to the officer in charge, give his name and the name and purpose of his group, and indicate how long the picket is expected to last. *Cooperation with the police is important.* It is best not to argue with them or ignore their orders. If on occasion they ask the picket to move back, tighten up, keep moving, or even move across the street, it is generally better to comply than to argue. As a rule, police restrictions will not harm the effectiveness of the picket, whereas disobeying their orders might lead to greater difficulties.

Apple Pie

Pickets are an old American tradition and are accepted everywhere. Some recent court rulings have been favorable to pickets and public demonstrations, allowing them to be carried out in some shopping centers. Rather than becoming outmoded or obsolete, the picket is more in vogue today than at almost any time in American history. It is one of the prolife movement's most effective tools.

In many cities the picket has effectively cut down on abortions, has led to lengthy discussions with clinic management and personnel, and has alerted the community and the press to the seriousness of the abortion controversy. It is difficult to ignore the presence of two or three hundred picketers at a clinic every week, vociferously claiming that human lives are being destroyed at the place being picketed. A picket is a necessary means of giving witness to the evil it tries to curb. Nearly anyone can join in a picket—old, young, children, couples, religious.

Promptness is vital to a good picket. Picketers must be advised to arrive on time. All directions and directives must be clear. If a picket is to start at a certain time, all leaders, marshals, and sign carriers should meet at a designated point beforehand, so that they will arrive at the picket site exactly on time. Nothing is more devastating to a picket than for picketers to arrive on time and find no leadership present. Some pickets have dissolved for this reason.

It is important to have someone in charge of handling the press. They should carry a set of press packets and hand these to all the media representatives. Also, have someone available to take down the name, address, and phone number of everyone who takes part in the picket. This serves several purposes. It gives you a list of people to call on in the future, because these are the people you can trust to come out. Second, you may want to send a letter afterward thanking those who took part and send them press clippings that have resulted from the picket. Third, it is good for people to know that their presence is not taken for granted, but that they are important to the cause. We never have trouble getting people to give their names. Someone with a clipboard simply walks along with each picketer until he has all the names and addresses. It may taken time, but it is a useful thing to do.

Two final comments: In every talk I give, I challenge Christians and other prolifers to search their consciences and ask why they do not spend at least two hours each month on a picket line, handing out literature or doing sidewalk counseling in front of an abortion clinic. I make two exceptions to this demand: cloistered nuns and federal prisoners serving life sentences. The challenge is open to everyone, from cardinal to judge, from governor to prolife author. I tell them to ask themselves if they are too important to do sidewalk work, to be a foot soldier in the battle for the unborn. I remind them that I know a cardinal who pickets, an archbishop, a Greek-Orthodox priest, a judge, a doctor, a police captain, and even a prolife lawyer. Are they superior to these? Are they too embarrased to save a human life?

Second, Franky Schaeffer has said that if there is an abortion clinic in your neighborhood and it is not picketed every time abortions are being performed there, that community has accepted abortion. To this excellent and powerful idea I would add only that if that situation exists, *you* have accepted abortion.

A large and well-organized picket will sometimes attract passersby who join when they learn the reason for the picket. In a celebrated picket in Indianapolis, early media coverage prompted some prolifers to drive across town to join the picket in progress, swelling the number to nearly three hundred, where only one hundred were anticipated. Work with local media or at least your local Christian radio station to promote the picket.

It is also wise to have counselors present at every abortion clinic picket. Picketing alone is effective, but it is more positive and helpful to have counselors present.

Checklist for Clinic Picket
Before the picket—

(1) Write and print leaflets or handouts to be used, explaining the purpose of the picket.

(2) Have an attorney review state and city laws governing picketing.

(3) Have phone numbers and addresses of all media—TV, radio, newspapers—to be contacted the morning of the picket.

(4) Check out the clinic for possible problems. Is it

in a shopping mall? What is the parking situation? What is the exact address?

(5) Get names and other facts about clinic personnel. Have they been or are they now being sued? Stress lawsuits in the leaflet to warn prospective clinics and inform the public.

(6) Make signs, using simple statements and large letters.

(7) Have a camera and film ready. Appoint a photographer.

(8) Notify police prior to the picket. Obtain a permit if necessary.

(9) Appoint spokesmen to talk to the press.

(10) Explain do's and don'ts to participants.

(11) Write and mail press releases.

During the picket—

(1) Avoid arguments or verbal battles with passersby. Step out of the picket line to discuss issues with others.

(2) Always be courteous. Do not shout back at hecklers.

(3) Obey the police as much as possible.

(4) Take pictures of the event for your files, newsletter, and follow-up stories.

(5) Use a bullhorn to maintain order.

(6) Alert the media by phone from the scene of the picket.

(7) Do not block pedestrians or auto traffic.

(8) Do not litter. Clean up afterward. If the public drops literature, they are littering, not you. The police cannot prevent you from distributing materials.

(9) If anyone is arrested, take pictures and get a tape recording of the procedure.

Why Violence Won't Work
There is a small fraction within the prolife movement— as there is within every social movement—who speak

from time to time about the need to stop abortion by more direct and forceful methods than are generally used. There are some who refer to the possibility of the abortion conflict escalating into a "shooting war."

Most of this sentiment is just talk. However, the fact remains that there have been some incidents of violence against both the prolife camp and the abortionists.

I have been struck, spit on, pushed, and have received innumerable death threats, warnings, insults, and crank calls. I have had my sight damaged, tires slashed, office windows cut with glass cutters and broken with rocks, and my office painted with roofing tar.

Nearly all prolife activist leaders can cite a similar list of threatening and violent acts. Some prolife offices have been fire-bombed. Prolife picketers and counselors have had buckets of water thrown on them, have had cars driven toward them at high speeds, have been struck with clubs by clinic guards, and have been subjected to a variety of insults and injuries.

On the other hand, there are a few highly publicized but questionable instances of what appear to be prolife harassment and violence against abortionists and their clinics. It should be pointed out that the abortionists, in presenting what they believe to be cases of prolife violence, rarely have evidence that an attack was made by prolife people. Moreover, they lump all manner of "events"— threatening telephone calls, bomb threats, and peaceful sit-ins—together, in an effort to present a sinister picture of prolife "terrorism." It should also be noted that it is ironic that those who live by violent means—the dismemberment of unborn children— should object to violence in others.

Nevertheless, all of the activist prolifers the Pro-Life Action League works with concur with the League's basic principle and program of *nonviolent direct action*. We take this program very seriously, believing that *violence on our part would be counterproductive and wrong*.

After all, it is the abortionists who are guilty of routine violence against unborn children (dismemberment, salt poisoning, strangulation) and against their mothers (hemmorhage, scarring, infection, sterility). Resorting to violence would damage the reputation of prolife activists and would suggest that traditional nonviolent methods do not work. *Use of violence would only reinforce the erroneous belief that the end justifies the means—that evil can be overcome by evil.* This is the abortionists' mentality, not ours.

Direct action and even peaceful civil disobedience have an important part to play in winning the prolife battle. *We believe violence does not.*

Let us use those peaceful means open to us now to stop abortion. If we do, we can change things *before* it comes to a violent confrontation. But the day is late. *Let us act to stop abortion now.*

7
Legislating Life
by David N. O'Steen and Darla St. Martin

Americans are creatures of law. Every two years seats in the most powerful Congress in the world are changed, with only rhetorical shots fired in the process. Every four years the single most important position in the secular world may change hands and the course of the entire nation may be altered, as it was in 1980, through the same orderly process of law.

Just as the leaders produced by this system are accepted for their term, so too, for the most part, are the laws and the ordinances that are generated. Perhaps it is a deeply ingrained sense of theoretical participation in the making of law that causes most citizens to instinctively acknowledge that obedience to the law is intrinsically good, even while knowing that they themselves stretch, bend, or break it at times. This is true even without the deterrent to breaking the law that is provided by penalties and punishments. However, those penalties are additional incentives for those who are essentially law-abiding. They provide a motivation to conform for those who do not regard the legislative process with particular esteem or feel bound to abide by the rules it generates.

The Law Teaches
Any beginning student of logic knows that while the converse of a proposition may be true or false, its truth or falsity has absolutely no logical relationship to the

truth or falsity of the original proposition. Unfortunately, many seem to forget this when dealing with morality and law. If what is illegal is "bad," then what is "good" must logically be legal. But that does not imply that the converse—that is, that what is legal must be good—is true.

Yet the false assumption that what is legal must be good, moral, or at least acceptable behavior seems to be deeply implanted in some national collective subconscious. That assumption is clearly responsible for much behavior in our secular society.

The other teaching aspect of law is its ability to force patterns of behavior. These forced patterns of behavior can, in a relatively short period of time, alter social attitudes that have been long established, even when these replaced customs and attitudes are very contrary to the ones replacing them.

This teaching aspect of the law can have tremendous effects. Today most of us drive around fifty-five miles per hour on the freeways, when just a few years ago most of us drove around seventy. The change of habit was not due solely to radar and unmarked squad cars.

A much more significant social change was produced by the public accommodations portion of the Civil Rights Act of 1964. In less than one generation it erased both the practice and the desire for the custom of rigid racial segregation which had permeated every aspect of Southern life for one hundred years since the War between the States. Today the South would no more return to that system than would any other part of the country, and many find it hard to even remember how the maintenance of segregated lunch counters, theatres, schools, and buses once played such a central role in Southern life. Martin Luther King, Jr., was correct in his prediction that once the law changed how people must act, their hearts would follow.

For those of us who wish to find practical methods

to save unborn babies from death by abortion, these two teaching aspects of law are of critical importance. The legal vacuum created by the United States Supreme Court's 1973 *Roe v. Wade* decision, which legalized abortion on demand, helps create the impression that abortion should be regarded as usual and proper, and its opponents as social deviants or fanatics. The problem is compounded by any positive laws that pattern social behavior toward the further acceptance of abortion, such as tax funding of abortion or funding of organizations that perform abortions. On the other hand, the psychological effect of law also makes it possible to pass restrictions on the custom of abortion, even in the context of *Roe v. Wade,* which have a deterrent and therefore life-saving impact far beyond the stated intent of the restriction.

Restrictions

Proabortion strategists clearly understand these dynamics and resist any restrictions, even when such resistance entails a short-term public relations disadvantage for them, as is the case in their opposition to parental notification laws. They realize that the sweeping proabortion victory of 1973, which came through judicial decree rather than through the legislative process, while placing prolife citizens at a decided legal disadvantage (and initiating a literal holocaust) also cheated abortion advocates of something. They were denied the true *legitimacy* a position gains when it endures and ultimately prevails in the rough-and-tumble politics of our democratic system. Civil rights have gained this legitimacy; abortion "rights" have not, yet.

In fact, a Gallup poll taken in late September 1984 showed that 50 percent of all Americans would support "a ban on all abortions except in cases of rape, incest or when the mother's life is endangered," while 45 percent opposed the ban and 5 percent had no opinion. According to testimony presented to the United States Senate

Constitution Subcommittee in October 1981, these three circumstances, together with danger to the mother's physical health or fetal handicap, collectively constitute the reasons for, at the very most, only 3 percent of the abortions performed.

Thus, a necessary strategy for the proabortion lobby is clearly evident: they must prevent any cracks in the fragile foundation of law protecting the "right" to abortion, while at the same time depending upon time and the instructional value of law to make that barbaric practice a permanent part of American culture.

The necessary prolife strategy in these circumstances is also clear. While under the yoke of *Roe v. Wade,* which essentially prevents state and federal legislative bodies from directly prohibiting abortion for any reason or at any time, it is crucial that prolife citizens continue to seek incremental restrictions on the practice of abortion which the courts will allow to stand. We must also seek new ways to test the court and focus public scrutiny on abortion on demand.

Such restrictions have three main results. First, they may immediately save lives. Second, they continue the public legal controversy surrounding abortion, which in turn has a deterrent effect on abortion itself and thus saves more lives. Finally, they teach the public that the law has not yet finished speaking on abortion and thereby help thwart the undesirable instructional effect of *Roe v. Wade* and its progeny. In other words, such restrictions force the public to at least subconsciously confront questions such as "If abortion is O.K., then why won't the government fund it?"

In addition, the process of passing restrictions that enjoy wide public support, such as abortion funding restrictions and parental notification laws, help expose the proabortion side's true unreasonable position. The process also helps prepare legislators for the actions they must take once *Roe v. Wade* is reversed.

Prolifers were tragically correct when they said in

the early seventies that the acceptance of abortion would logically lead to the acceptance of death as a solution to the problems of other vulnerable groups, such as the newborn and the aged. The Baby Doe cases made the reality of infanticide public. Moreover, the emergence of a wide variety of "right-to-die" legislative proposals must be viewed with alarm. Thus, the prolife legislative agenda must also include protection of these other threatened elements of humankind.

Of course, a major goal of the right-to-life movement is to reverse *Roe v. Wade* and make possible direct legislative protection for unborn children. *Roe v. Wade* could be reversed through a constitutional amendment, or through changes in the Supreme Court to establish a majority who would interpret the Constitution according to its actual text and history. The prospects for such a reversal will be enhanced only by continued prolife legislative activity at both the state and federal levels within the parameters allowed by the courts at any given time.

Knowing what must be done and doing it are different things. To the prolife citizens who have toiled within the system for a dozen years, the results often seemed mixed, and the process has brought frustration and real tears. At times it seems insane to plan strategy, write letters, and rationally discuss with legislators whether or not society should allow innocent children to be put to death by abortion (knowing that even as we plan and write and lobby, babies are still dying at the rate of about one every twenty seconds).

Such thoughts and feelings often came to those working at the office of Minnesota Citizens Concerned for Life. On the same street as the office, one of the nation's early advocates and practitioners of dilation and evacuation (or D & E abortions) plied her deadly trade. This grisly method involves literally hacking apart second-trimester babies by alternating attacks from suction and scraping. Yet, this woman was only one of thousands of executioners, and her victims only a minute fraction of the millions who have died, or may be destined to die, because of the travesty of law that protects such slaughter.

As prolife activists, we want to save every single child possible; but our purpose must be to save millions in this and future generations. That will happen only if the legal aberration that placed abortion in the mainstream of our culture, and made the consideration of infanticide and euthanasia respectable, is ended.

Strategic Planning

Saving the children, and perhaps the human race, requires more than voices, sorrow, or anger. It requires strategic planning, coordination, and a little finesse. It also requires the perseverance to continue despite the emotions and feelings of frustration often felt by any sensitive person who understands the reality of the situation that has existed since 1973.

Have prolife legislative efforts since 1973, and the organizational development work such efforts have necessitated, actually saved lives? Definitely. In the first year following the implementation of Minnesota's parental notification law on abortion, the number of teenage abortions dropped by approximately nine hundred. As long as that law remains in effect, it will keep saving lives. All of us who worked to pass that bill could have shaken our fists from dawn to dusk at the abortion mill down the street from the MCCL office, and we never would have had the impact gained by our efforts to pass that law.

Clearly the work of the many citizens who built the one hundred and fifty MCCL chapters that reach into every legislative district, and almost every precinct, of that state has not been in vain. In the climate of the legislative atmosphere they have created, it is no accident that liberal Minnesota, which has an active proabortion movement, also has one of the lowest abortion rates in the country. Of the fifty largest metropolitan areas in the U.S., Minneapolis has the seventh lowest number of abortion clinics per one hundred thousand women.

On a much larger scale, the total number of abortions performed nationally each year, which predictably doubled between the first years following the Supreme Court's blessing and the end of the 1970s, actually leveled off in the early 1980s and in some localities declined. A large part of this must be attributed to the psychology created by continued state and national prolife legislative strategy and activity which has denied abortion all of the legitimacy the law usually bestows. Without a doubt, this has caused many thousands of mothers to hesitate and many thousands of children to be born. We may never know just who they are, but the lives saved are real nonetheless.

Legislation

Lives have been saved, but more remains to be done. Since 1973 the right-to-life movement has identified areas of legislative involvement which have, at least on a partial basis, withstood court tests and produced meaningful results. Of course, success requires a coordinated effort. Thus, prolife citizens should first become part of their state right-to-life organization and their local chapter.

If your state right-to-life organization doesn't have a chapter in your area, help start one. Then find out the legislative history of your state in the life areas and your state organization's plans for the current session. The state organization can in turn coordinate its efforts with the National Right-To-Life Committee (NRLC), which is made up of statewide groups in all fifty states, as well as with other national organizations such as the National

Committee for a Human Life Amendment (NCHLA), which has grass-root groups in most congressional districts. Both NRLC and NCHLA are based in Washington, D.C.

Following is a discussion of some of the areas of current prolife legislative activity. This is not intended to be all-inclusive, but rather gives a brief discussion of some of the principal areas. Of course, changes in the way the courts view the unborn child, abortion, and the Constitution may continue to expand this list until direct legal protection can be restored by legislative action.

Abortion Funding Restrictions
Since 1977 the United States Supreme Court has recognized that both federal and state governments have a right *not* to fund abortions. Federal activity in this area has included annual reenactment of the Hyde Amendment to the appropriations bill. This currently limits Medicaid abortion funding to life-of-mother cases. Similar "riders" have also been used to restrict federal funding of abortion within other federal programs such as the Peace Corps and the military. The restrictions of abortion funding within the military have now been made a part of statutory law which does not have to be renewed annually. A goal for the right-to-life movement is to enact a similar statutory provision covering Medicaid and eliminating the need for the annual appropriations rider.

Federal law also disallows the direct use of foreign aid population control funds or domestic family planning funds for abortion. However, federal funding of organizations that perform abortions with funds obtained from other sources remains a problem. In two instances, courts have not allowed states to restrict the use of state family planning money to nonabortion providers. However, it seems that the federal government has greater latitude in so restricting the use of federal funds in foreign countries. At the Mexico City Conference on World Population held in the summer of 1984, the United States announced a policy of denying funds to private international groups that "perform or actively promote" abortion.

Use of state funds to pay for abortions varies greatly from state to state. Some states fund essentially any abortion under their medical assistance program. Some restrict abortion funding to life-of-mother cases only, while others restrict abortion to cases such as life, rape, and incest. Some of the rape and incest exceptions are tightly drawn. Two states allow funding in these circumstances only in cases of forced rape which are reported to law enforcement agencies within forty-eight hours, or in incest cases where the aggressor is reported to law enforcement agencies.

If your state does not currently restrict abortion funding, that should be one top priority of your state right-to-life movement. However, activity should be carefully coordinated by the state organization for success.

In 1984, Colorado successfully passed a state referendum restricting abortion funding. In Washington a similar measure was narrowly defeated, and in Arkansas one was taken off the ballot by that state's supreme court. Experiences with referendums have shown that they should be entered only after very careful planning and coordination with the national right-to-life movement. In a small state, a minimum of $300,000 to $500,000 appears necessary for such an effort due to the enormous funding that the proabortion industry can feed to the media to misrepresent and defeat such a referendum, not to mention the free media they may get to support their side.

It should be noted that defeat of a prolife referendum may be very harmful to prolife support in that state's legislative and congressional delegation. This is another reason referendums should be approached with caution.

Related to the area of abortion funding is the question of state or federal payment for employees' health insurance policies that provide for elective abortion. At the federal level, the Smith-Denton amendment currently prohibits the use of federal funds to provide abortion coverage in federal employees' health insurance plans. Like the Hyde amendment, this rider must currently be renewed annually and is not now part of statutory law. Similar legislation regarding state employees may be feasible in some states that have already restricted direct payment for abortions.

All of these measures are an important part of keeping government out of the abortion business and play a significant role in illegitimatizing the practice' of abortion. Polls have also shown that strong majorities disapprove of abortion funding. Therefore, legislative activity in this area also serves to place the proabortion lobby at a disadvantage and gives prolife organizations useful voting records.

Parental Notification and/or Consent
In a case involving Massachusetts law, the United States Supreme Court recognized parental consent restrictions on abortions performed on minors with certain provisions. Those provisions include a stipulation that the girl must have an option of going into court and that the court must allow the abortion without parental consent if the abortion is in the girl's "best interest" or if the girl is sufficiently "mature" to make the decision on her own.

Parental notification and consent laws do save some lives. As indicated, teenage abortions dropped by approximately nine hundred annually when Minnesota's parental notification law went into effect.

While the judicial override provisions would appear to have the potential for nullifying the intended effect of such laws, since some judges would routinely authorize abortions without notification or consent, in practice these provisions may not be as troublesome as first thought. Especially in the case of notification, the teenager may well decide that it is easier in the end just to notify her parents than to go into court with the possibility that the court will ultimately require notification anyway.

Once parents are notified, this creates the potential for dialogue between them and their daughter. Such dialogue may produce understanding and alternatives which the daughter had not anticipated, and another life may be saved.

Parental notification bills are excellent devices for engaging proabortion forces in debate. Polls consistently show overwhelming public support for these measures, and by opposing them abortion advocates again show how unreasonable they really are.

Health Insurance and HMO's

Prolife citizens should find out if their state requires that health insurance plans covering maternity benefits also cover abortion. If so, legislation can be sought to allow insurance policies to be bought and sold within that state that do not pay for elective abortions, but do provide maternity benefits. This is really a freedom-of-conscience provision and helps segregate abortion as a deviant practice.

Citizens should also find out if health maintenance organization (HMO) plans in their state require abortion coverage. (This is a generic term for a wide variety of prepaid medical care.) If so, legislation can be sought to stipulate that HMO's without elective abortion coverage can be bought and sold within the state.

Unisex Insurance

There has been some activity in Congress regarding the possibility of legislation to make any distinction in insurance policies on the basis of sex illegal. A consensus exists among prolife legal scholars that this would probably have the effect of requiring elective abortion coverage within health insurance policies. Any such legislation should be amended to specifically allow health insurance policies to be sold with maternity coverage, but without coverage for elective abortion.

Conscience Clauses

Another aspect of keeping abortion isolated from mainstream society to the greatest degree possible is to provide that hospitals and hospital personnel have the right to refuse to perform, assist with, or accommodate abortions. In 1973 and 1977 the Supreme Court recognized the right of hospitals *not* to perform abortions. This right has been widely accepted among private hospitals, and the 1977 Supreme Court case dealt with a publicly owned hospital. (One publicly owned hospital is currently under lower court order to perform abortions, but that case is not binding elsewhere.)

Forty-four states have enacted legislation to protect the rights of conscience of hospital personnel, but compliance with these laws should be monitored. This means that local prolife groups must be organized and must coordinate their activities with national prolife groups.

Fetal Experimentation

Fetal experimentation legislation is intended to prevent the use of children who survive abortions as experimental subjects (unless experimental treatment is actually intended to help the child) and to prevent nontherapeutic experimentation on unborn children intended for abortion. In the latter case, such experimentation may involve subjecting the child to chemicals and drugs in order to examine the dead body following the abortion for deformities or other harmful effects induced by the substance.

Besides such legislation's humanitarian value, its passage helps force public recognition of the unborn child as a human being.

Current federal regulations restrict the use of federal funds for nontherapeutic fetal experimentation. However, over two-thirds of the states still permit such harmful experiments, and protective legislation is needed in these.

Wrongful Life/Wrongful Birth Statutes

The need for this type of legislation has arisen from suits that have been brought on behalf of either parents or children, claiming that the child's life was wrongfully allowed to continue or that he was wrongfully born due to the negligence of another. Such suits have generally been brought in cases where handicapped children were born and the parents claimed that if they had been properly informed of the possibility of such handicap, they would have aborted the child. Implicit in such suits is the contention that the lives of such handicapped children are not worth living and that they would have been better off aborted.

Besides the totally unacceptable philosophical premise on which such suits are based, they have the practical effect of creating a climate of fear in which physicians, in order to avoid lawsuits, may feel they must encourage abortions in all cases where there is any possibility of fetal handicaps. Clearly this would cost many lives.

At least two states, Minnesota and South Dakota, have passed legislation stating that no one may collect damages against another on the grounds that the other's actions, or lack of actions, caused a child to be wrongfully born. This protects physicians from being sued because they do not recommend abortions.

This legislation is extremely important. It not only helps protect children who are suspected of possible handicap, but it also denies the claims that there are lives not worth living and that parents have a positive right to have handicapped children killed.

ERA

Prolife attorneys have feared for some time that the Equal Rights Amendment, as originally drafted for both the federal and state constitutions, would be interpreted to require public funding of abortion. While proabortion lobbyists have denied any ERA/abortion connection before legislative bodies, in several suits against state abortion funding restrictions in states where ERAs had also passed, proabortion attorneys have argued that the state ERA does require public abortion funding.

In 1984 a Pennsylvania court ruled that that state's ERA alone was sufficient to strike Pennsylvania's law restricting abortion funding. That decision was later overturned by another court, but it is still on appeal. Moreover, regardless of its final disposition, this case indicates that any ERA legislation that is not explicitly made neutral regarding abortion poses a grave threat to hard-won abortion funding restrictions.

Prolife organizations should oppose any federal ERA that is not amended to be neutral on abortion. The abortion neutralization amendment to an ERA law would read: "Nothing in this article shall be construed to want and secure any right relating to abortion or the funding thereof." Such language should be added to any ERA at the state or federal level.

In 1984 prolife citizens in Maine succeeded in defeating a referendum for an ERA that was not amended to be neutral on abortion. The cost for prolife efforts in that referendum was over $300,000.

Baby Doe Legislation

In April 1982 a newborn, handicapped, Down's syndrome child, known in court records as Baby Doe, was allowed to starve to death and was denied medical treatment in a hospital in Bloomington, Indiana. Since that time the prolife movement has recognized the need for both state and federal legislative protection for newborn handicapped children.

After the courts thwarted the Reagan administration's early attempts to provide some protection through regulations based on then existing laws, an initial Baby Doe measure was enacted by Congress in the summer of 1984. This has the effect of defining the denial of routine medical care to handicapped newborns as child abuse for the purpose of the federal Child Abuse Act. This law places upon state agencies the responsibility to identify and protect such children within the parameter of that act and provides funding at both the state and federal level to train agencies to properly implement it. This important measure is but a first step in building the necessary framework of state and federal law to protect these vulnerable children from neglect. Some states, such as Indiana, have passed state legislation in this area, and such legislation is needed in those states that have not yet acted.

Euthanasia and Death Legislation
On another front, prolife citizens and organizations need to carefully monitor any legislation which might become a step toward the practice of euthanasia or the denial of human rights and needed medical care to the aged and critically ill. Dangerous legislation in this area should meet prolife resistance and defeat. Any proposed legislation bearing titles such as Living Will, Definition of Death, or Right-to-Die should come under immediate prolife scrutiny.

Human Life Amendments
Since 1973 a goal of the prolife movement has been to reverse the *Roe v. Wade* decision by a constitutional amendment which would make possible legislation pro-

tecting the unborn and, hopefully, even establish within the Constitution mandatory protection for the unborn and all human life.

In the summer of 1983 the United States Senate voted on a constitutional amendment proposed by Senator Orrin Hatch, a human life amendment which would have reversed *Roe v. Wade* and made possible legislation directly prohibiting abortion. The amendment failed on a vote of forty-nine for, fifty against, and one abstention.

The hearings which led to the vote on the Hatch amendment were of tremendous educational value. The amendment also gave prolife political action committees their first clear up or down vote on abortion on demand in the United States Senate in ten years.

Following the 1984 elections, the United States Senate remained essentially evenly divided on such an amendment. An amendment that would directly mandate legal protection probably has somewhat less support in the Senate.

There may be a majority, but not the necessary two-thirds, for either type of amendment in the House of Representatives. However, any human life amendment is currently stalled in hostile House committees, as has been the case since 1973.

A human life amendment remains an ultimate goal of the prolife movement. However, other means to reverse *Roe v. Wade* and make possible direct legal protection may become feasible before a human life amendment is possible. In fact, the chances for an ideal amendment establishing a standard of protection within the Constitution may be strengthened if legislation prohibiting abortion first becomes permissible. This is true since such legislation would fundamentally alter public perception of the unborn under the law.

Legislation to Reverse *Roe v. Wade*
When the Supreme Court reaffirmed *Roe v. Wade* in 1983, Justice Sandra Day O'Connor issued a strong dis-

sent (in which she was joined by Justices White and Rehnquist). If President Reagan in his second term replaces at least two proabortion justices with jurists who will respect human life and interpret the Constitution according to its text and history, then Court-enforced abortion on demand may be ended.

Since the abandonment of *Roe v. Wade* may come in a sequence of partial reversals, it is important to have new legislative tests of its validity prepared for the Court to consider at the right time. The best test or sequence of tests may depend on the composition of the new Court.

The System

The passage of legislation is a complex process, and prolifers can more effectively master it if they understand how their government functions.

The American political system divides the power of government into three branches—the executive, the legislative, and the judicial. All three branches are important for the prolife cause. The chief executive signs legislation, directs the government, and appoints judges. The judicial branch judges the constitutionality of laws and tries offenders. Recently, however, some judges have usurped the power of the legislative branch and have "legislated from the bench" by handing down decisions based more on their personal opinion of what the law ought to be than on any strict interpretation of the law or the Constitution. The United States Supreme Court abortion decision is one of the most obvious cases of "legislating from the bench." Thus, the appointment of prolife judges must be one of the movement's goals.

In the Constitution, the legislative branch is charged with the primary responsibility for making the laws. The process used varies slightly from state to state and between the state and federal level. However, the major steps are:

(1) A bill is entered in one house by its authors. Usually an identical bill is also entered in the other house.

(2) The bill is assigned to a committee or committees in both houses.

(3) The committee chairman may assign the bill to a subcommittee.

(4) In most bodies the committee and/or the subcommittee chairman has the power to either schedule the bill for a hearing or let the bill die in the committee without further action.

(5) If the bill gets a hearing, the body hears testimony from interested parties.

(6) The bill is then considered by the committee and any amendments are voted upon.

(7) If the bill is passed by a subcommittee, it goes back to the full committee.

(8) The full committee chairman must then schedule it for consideration.

(9) The full committee members also have the opportunity to amend the bill and then vote to pass or defeat it. If the bill passes out of committee, it goes to the full body.

(10) In most bodies the legislative leadership (the Speaker or majority leader or a committee of legislative leaders) has the critical power to schedule legislation on the calendar.

(11) When the bill reaches the floor, it is debated and any amendments are added.

(12) Finally there is a vote on the floor.

(13) If it passes, the bill has to go through the whole process again in the other house.

(14) If there are any differences in the versions of the bill passed by the two houses, a conference committee must meet and resolve the differences.

(15) The version of the bill which emerges from the conference committee must then be passed by both

houses. (If it is not, it then goes back to the conference committee for further changes and then returns to both houses again.)

(16) After both houses have passed the same version of the bill, it goes to the Chief Executive for his signature.

(17) The executive can either sign it or veto it.

(18) Usually a veto can be overridden by a two-thirds vote in both houses.

(19) If the bill survives all of these steps and is signed into law, the Supreme Court may still declare it unconstitutional.

Supreme Court decisions can be reversed by the Supreme Court itself or by a constitutional amendment. The amendment itself must pass through the same process as a bill, except that it must pass both houses with a two-thirds vote. Then, instead of an executive's signature, it is sent to the states for ratification. Three-fourths of the states must ratify it before it becomes part of the Constitution. The Constitution itself can be interpreted by the Supreme Court. However, the Constitution and all its amendments are by definition constitutional.

The American political system is one in which we as citizens have both the opportunity and the power to affect change. Amending the Constitution of the United States or obtaining a reversal of a Supreme Court decision by the Court itself may be long and difficult processes. But the fact is that such legislation is really possible!

With determined, effective citizen action, ordinary people can change the course of American history. However, it will require years of real dedication to reverse the Supreme Court's abortion decision.

Some people who were trained for other careers will be called instead to be professionals in the prolife movement. Many people who had planned other lives must instead devote a large part of their time to work for the lives of children. And literally millions must contribute in some way. Without the sacrifices—large and small—of all these good people, there will be no protection for the children in this century.

Even dedication and determination, however, must be directed intelligently to be successful. Prolife people must understand not only how the American political system works, but also how they can most effectively impact it, both as organized groups and as individuals.

Abortion on demand for the entire nine months of pregnancy became the law of the land on January 22, 1973, when the United States Supreme Court overturned all protective state abortion laws for the entire nation. The Supreme Court abortion decision can be reversed only by another decision by the Court itself or by a constitutional amendment.

Supreme Court Justices are appointed for life by the President. Thus, it is important that we choose Presidents who include respect of the lives and rights of unborn children as one of the basic criteria necessary for appointment to the Supreme Court.

This is not an unreasonable criterion. Several Presidents have required a belief in the equality of opportunity for black citizens as a basic criterion. The right to life of unborn children is also a basic right and should receive the same consideration.

Moreover, since a constitutional amendment must be proposed by two-thirds of both houses for Congress and then passed by three-fourths of the states, prolifers need to work on both the state and federal level.

In the meantime, legislation to impact abortion that can be passed on both the state and federal level serves a dual role. It impacts abortion immediately, while also giving prolifers the necessary experience and test votes to build toward a constitutional amendment someday.

How all of this can be practically accomplished organizationally and individually needs more detailed explanation.

The Prolife Network

The proabortion movement is a formidable force in American society. Proabortionists acquired a multimillion dollar international organization when they took over a respected existing group promoting family planning, Planned Parenthood. Persons who did not favor abortion were eliminated from Planned Parenthood, and advocacy of abortion became its chief focus.

The newly developing feminist movement, originally advocating only equal opportunities for women, was also seized by proabortionists who drove out prolife women and excluded them from positions in the feminist organizations. They demanded that only women who pledged to support the Supreme Court abortion decision could serve.

Now both feminist and "family planning" groups have made abortion a top priority, to the great detriment of the original purposes of their movements. With their numerous allies in the press, these two groups constitute a powerful force.

That force can be countered, but only with a well-organized counter force. Prolifers, however, have had to build their groups from the ground up. There have been no short cuts—no multimillion dollar groups to take over and turn into single-minded advocates. The task is difficult, but together we are equal to it.

It is essential that there be large, well-organized, national prolife groups. Only such groups can provide the permanent professional staff to plan long-term strategy and carry out the interrelated integrated action necessary on the national level in the many important aspects of prolife work.

The national groups also need well-organized statewide affiliate groups with full-time staff persons in every state, as well as local affiliates in communities throughout the nation.

There must be prolife groups working closely with the state and national groups in every community in this country if we are going to meet the challenges of this decade. However, we must recognize that these are no substitute for large, central, nationwide organizations that can really counter the proabortion giants.

Building our own effective prolife network will take the efforts of many in several major areas: organization, education, and legislation.

Organization is, of course, the foundation of building any group. Identifying and activating fellow-prolifers on every level lays the groundwork for all the other activities. Hundreds of thousands of people are needed. Whether on the national, state, or local level, every additional prolifer added to the group brings another involved person into the movement to carry out prolife work.

Education is another important prolife activity. Both prolife groups and individuals can educate in literally thousands of ways. With the media generally hostile to the prolife message, it is essential to have a group in every state and community to get prolife information out to the public and to take advantage of every opportunity to publicize the facts about life, death, and abortion. The local group can provide press releases, place ads, buy radio time, volunteer to speak at churches, schools, and events, provide books and brochures, and generally serve as the source of prolife resources.

Excellent educational materials and techniques have been developed over the past ten years, ranging from simple brochures to the latest multimedia technology. A new local group does not need to re-invent everything. By affiliating with national prolife groups, they can immediately benefit from years of development and experience.

Legislation—passing effective laws to protect the un-

born—is the key to saving the children. Prolifers must be willing to participate in the political process and learn to take full advantage of the opportunities citizens have to make their voices heard by government. To impact legislation, they must also have access to accurate information in time to affect decision-making.

Here the closely-knit organizational network of prolife groups on local, state, and national levels is more necessary than ever. Democracy works on a tight time schedule. Critical legislation can come up in a state legislature or in Congress with little advance notice. The most persuasive letter or call appealing for a legislator's vote is worthless after the vote is over.

Prolife groups must provide the network to keep prolifers throughout the nation informed on what is going on in their legislative bodies and what they, as citizens, can do about it. Nowhere else can prolifers obtain this information. The mass media provide only erratic, distorted information on the prolife issue. Therefore, the regular flow of legislative information through the prolife national network is absolutely critical.

When prolife groups first entered the legislative arena, they began by trying to persuade their representatives to support prolife legislation or defeat proabortion legislation. However, it soon became obvious that there were some legislators who could not be counted on to vote prolife. Prolife citizens then began to request information on legislative voting records. To meet the need, prolife groups began to publish regularly the voting records of legislators and Congressmen.

But prolifers still needed a method of predicting how new candidates for office would vote if elected. Thus, the candidate questionnaire was born. Prolife groups asked candidates a series of questions about abortion, euthanasia, and infanticide and published the answers in their newsletters. This gave prolife individuals the necessary information to take intelligent action.

It was in the late 1970s before prolife groups took

the step of actually becoming involved in the election process as groups. Like many advocacy groups, prolife groups formed their own political action committees (PACs). By 1980 the prolife movement was a real political force to be reckoned with.

All of these activities gave the prolife movement great legislative and political potential, but none of it has happened without the dedicated efforts of thousands of prolifers sacrificing their time and funds to build organizations for unborn children. In all these areas the efforts must continue. Individual prolifers giving what they can of time, talent, and money are crucial to the success of our mission.

The Individual
Joining and directly helping to build a prolife national group network is a major priority. However, there are many specific individual activities which can also help reach the goal.

Each of you reading this can make your own personal contribution to ending the abortion holocaust.

You can:

(1) Join the various national prolife organizations, statewide right-to-life groups, and affiliated community right-to-life groups.

(2) Support these groups financially to the best of your own ability.

(3) Help to organize a local community prolife group or, if there is already one, help to develop and expand it.

(4) Write letters to the editor for the prolife cause.

(5) Telephone or write newspapers, magazines, or television stations to protest reporting that is biased against the prolife cause.

(6) Keep informed about the prolife issue and educate the people you meet every day.

(7) Always respond immediately to legislative alerts

with a letter, phone call, or a personal visit to your legislator.

(8) Try to develop a speaking acquaintance with the public officials who represent you. Only the President is inaccessible to the average citizen who is willing to exert a little effort. You can personally meet even your governor or senator if you are persistent enough and go to events where they are present. Every prolife citizen who speaks out serves to remind a public official of the importance of the prolife issue to his or her constituents.

(9) Work on the campaign of a prolife candidate, and make certain you build a personal relationship with him or her. The people who work on a candidate's campaign have more influence on that candidate later and can help to line up critical votes when there is heavy pressure on prolife officials to stray on a vote.

(10) Get acquainted with the other people around your public officials, who also influence them. These may include family, friends, and pastors for local officials, and staff for higher officials. Educate these people on prolife issues too. (The proabortionists have developed the technique of trying to reach the wives of male public officials and using them to influence their husbands.)

(11) Vote prolife. Find out where the candidates stand on abortion, and make abortion a disqualifying issue. This means that anyone who will not support equal protection for unborn children has disqualified himself from receiving your vote.

(12) Remember that what you say about the prolife issue itself is not the only way in which you convey a prolife message. People will also judge the prolife movement and the validity of its position by the caring attitude of concern you display toward all human beings, even those who disagree with you.

(13) Be alert for opportunities to use the other groups to which you belong to help the prolife cause.

Some groups need educating on the issue. Others are already strongly prolife and can be asked to provide volunteers or a financial contribution.

(14) Each person is unique. Use your own special talents and opportunities to defend life whenever and however you can. Have the courage and dedication to act even when it requires self-sacrifice.

Meeting the Challenge
The task is a challenge to each of us individually and to the prolife movement collectively. We can and must meet that challenge because we are in a fundamental struggle over the value of human beings and their right to equality and justice.

Whatever the outcome, the struggle itself will alter the course of human history. Each of us has the opportunity and the responsibility to play an important role in that struggle.

PART THREE:
Conclusion

8
People Make a Difference
by John W. Whitehead

People make a difference. This is what this book is all about.

No matter your profession or form of employment. No matter your age or education. You can make a difference.

You can save lives. You can change history. Everything you do is significant.

Our business, then, should be a people business. Our main concern in our secular age must be the care and love of people. This, of course, runs against the grain of modern culture. Nevertheless, it must be a central concern of all those who love life and liberty.

The innocent child, nestled inside his mother's womb, is dependent upon us for his life. The child with Down's syndrome is dependent on us for continuing life. The elderly person on a life support system is dependent on us.

The burden is great, but it is an honor to bear such a burden. It is the burden of caring and loving people. This is the essence of true religion.

The task before us may seem overwhelming. However, since what people do is significant, we can change things. Already, since the 1973 *Roe v. Wade* decision, the prolife movement has saved thousands of children.

The great battle of our time—the destruction of human life—can be won if we in the prolife movement work together. This means discarding personalities and, if need be, subordinating egos and organizations to the interest of saving lives. Building bureaucratic prolife organizations and personalities will mean nothing if we do not arrest abortion.

I am convinced that our generation will be judged according to its response to abortion, infanticide, and euthanasia. It will do no good on Judgment Day if we can say that we were only superficially opposed to abortion or that we prayed that it be stopped. It will do no good if we did not act.

To be effective, we must counsel, open pregnancy crisis centers and LIGHT Houses, picket, demonstrate, and do all the things suggested in the preceding pages. We must care. *We must act.*

Therefore, let us join hands in our important struggle. Let us not stand on the sidelines. Instead, may we get into the flow of history and act for "the least of these."

Notes

Editor's Foreword

1. "Sterilization Leads Birth Control List; Popularity Exceeds Pill's," *Washington Post* (Dec. 6, 1984), p. A6.

Chapter One: Decision Time

1. *Whatever Happened to the Human Race?* is available as a five-part film series from Gospel Films, Inc. 2735 E. Apple Ave., Muskegon, MI 49443. The companion book by Francis A. Schaeffer and Dr. C. Everett Koop was originally published by Fleming H. Revell and is now available in paperback from Crossway Books, Westchester, IL.

2. See the book *Death in the Nursery* by James Manney and John C. Blattner (Ann Arbor, MI: Servant Books, 1984). In particular, see Chapter 1, "The Untold Story of Infant Doe."

3. The paper most outspoken in advocating infanticide before the question became widely publicized appeared in the 167-year-old prestigious *New England Journal of Medicine* in October 1973. The proinfanticide paper was titled, "Moral and Ethical Dilemmas in the Special Care Nursery," by Dr. Raymond S. Duff and Dr. A. G. M. Campbell of the Department of Pediatrics at Yale University School of Medicine.

4. *Roe v. Wade,* January 1973, the majority opinion written by Justice Blackmun, striking down the antiabortion laws nationwide and providing abortion on demand up to the day of birth, qualifying only in the last trimester that abortion can be prevented except in cases where the

health or *mental health* of the mother is at stake, thereby leaving abortion on demand totally open.

5. *Op. cit., Death in the Nursery,* pp. 10, 11.

6. In March 1983, less than a year after the death of Infant Doe, the Department of Health and Human Services (HHS) issued the first version of what was soon to be known as the "Baby Doe Regulations." The regulations were based on Section 504 of the 1973 Rehabilitation Act. See pages 135-139 of *op. cit., Death in the Nursery.*

7. As soon as the Baby Doe HHS regulations were in place, a coalition of medical groups, led by the American Academy of Pediatrics, filed a lawsuit in federal court aimed at overturning them. Efforts to stop, curb, or regulate infanticide have been consistently opposed by the American Medical Association as well. For further details see *op. cit., Death in the Nursery,* pp. 136-144.

8. The idea that there is such a thing as a life not worthy to be lived has been studied and compared by Leo Alexander, psychiatrist for the prosecution at the Nuremburg Trials, to the original Nazi eugenics movement which sought to eliminate the handicapped and infirm before it turned toward questions of "racial purity" and began hounding and killing the Jews.

9. The first effort we know of in this country to educate the medical profession in the art of infanticide was a documentary motion picture titled, "Who Shall Survive?" Johns Hopkins Hospital and Medical School produced it in 1972. It shows a newborn infant with Downs syndrome, frequently called Mongolism, who was permitted to die by "inattention." See *op. cit., Whatever Happened to the Human Race?,* pp. 29-31.

10. *Op. cit., New England Journal of Medicine,* October 1973.

11. A study of pediatricians and obstetricians in the San Francisco Bay area found that 22 percent favored active or passive euthanasia in cases of Downs syndrome babies with no complication. If the baby also had an intestinal obstruction, 50 percent would withhold surgery and let the baby die. The study director commented that "some physicians chose to view a relatively simple operation as an insurmountable barrier." A survey of physicians' atti-

tudes which appeared in the *Hastings Center Report,* April 1976, p. 2, "Treating the Defective Newborn."

12. A study which appeared in *Pediatrics Magazine,* Vol. 60, Number 4, Part 2, October 1977, pp. 588-599, by Anthony Shaw, et al., "Ethical Issues in Pediatric Surgery: A National Survey of Pediatricians and Pediatric Surgeons." This was a scientifically sound study. The survey was well-designed, and response rate was high. The results are reliable. In all, 267 pediatric surgeons and 190 pediatricians answered questions about how they would deal with medical ethical issues that arose in the treatment of handicapped disabled newborns.

13. In October 1983, a group of Oklahoma physicians published a paper in *Pediatrics* describing a selection process whereby they decided not to operate on twenty-four spina bifida babies. The unlucky infants were transferred to a suburban home converted to an "intermediate care" facility where they were fed but not treated with antibiotics to attack the inevitable infections. Not surprisingly, all twenty-four babies died. The authors of the article revealing this study were four physicians from the University of Oklahoma Health Science Center and a social worker from Oklahoma Children's Memorial Hospital. The authors described in detail how their "selection committee" worked and what its results had been.

14. *Christianity Today* magazine, for instance, has had no cover story at the date of this writing on infanticide, despite their secular counterparts treating the issue, in many instances, as a higher priority.

15. Pope John Paul II has spoken out consistently on this matter, as have his newly appointed American bishops, most notably Bernard Law of Boston. Even the "liberal" bishops, such as Cardinal Bernardin of Chicago, have maintained a strong position on this issue.

16. *Brave New People* by D. Gareth Jones (Downers Grove, IL: InterVarsity Press, 1984, recalled; Grand Rapids, MI: Eerdmans, 1984). Consider the following from page 177:

And yet there are sometimes family situations where inadequacy, marital breakdown, financial stringency, unemployment and a host of other adverse social conditions could lead to the conclusion that abortion of an unwanted pregnancy, or of a pregnancy with a dubious outcome [i.e., genetic defects discovered through amniocentesis screening] is the least tragic of a number of tragic options.

17. *Ibid*, p. 181:

Abortion, especially for therapeutic reasons, confronts Christians with the agony of sometimes having to choose between what they recognize as the ideal—protection of fetal life—and what may seem inevitable in some circumstances—the destruction of fetal life. For those Christians who find themselves in counseling and obstetric situations, this is an invidious choice to have to make. Some may argue that it should never be made. . . . While respecting the integrity of those arguing in this way, I am unhappy with this course of action because it refuses to come to terms with all the relationships of which the woman seeking a therapeutic abortion is part.

On page 182 we find:

The factors which have to be weighed up when contemplating a therapeutic abortion are relative ones. Christians with a high view of life will emphasize the preservation of life and yet will also take into account the mental, spiritual and financial resources of the family and also the availabilty of social and welfare services for handicapped children in the community.

18. Carl F. H. Henry's book is titled *The Christian Mindset in a Secular Society* (Portland: Multnomah Press, 1984). On page 103 we find the following:

The fetus seems less than human, moreover, in cases of extreme deformity in which rational and moral capacities integral to the *imago Dei* are clearly lacking.

In such cases Carl Henry tells us that abortion is permissible.

19. Letha Scanzoni and Nancy Hardesty, writing in *All We're Meant to Be* (Waco, TX: Word Books, 1975):

What about a Christian couple who learn through genetic counseling that tests show their baby will be mongoloid, or the wife who contracts rubella early in her pregnancy and knows her child is likely to be malformed? Does Christian morality insist that these pregnancies be carried through, even though bringing the child into the world may cause extreme emotional distress and financial hardships for the family? We think not.

20. See Paul Johnson's book, *Modern Times* (New York: Harper & Row, 1983).

21. See *The Spirit of Democratic Capitalism* by Michael Novak (New York: Simon & Schuster, 1983), particularly his arguments on liberation and the church officials participating in the Sandinista regime in Nicaragua.

22. For instance, Governor Richard Lamm of Colorado said, "People who die without having their lives artifically extended are similar to leaves falling off a tree and forming humus for the other plants to grow up. You've got a duty to die and get out of the way. Let the other society, our kids, build a reasonable life." In the *San Jose Mercury News*, March 28, 1984.

23. See numerous articles in *Pediatrics* magazine and other medical journals arguing in favor of infanticide in various forms, especially one by medical ethicist Peter Singer, "Sanctity of Life or Quality of Life?," *Pediatrics*, July 1983:

Once the religious mumbo-jumbo surrounding the term "human" has been stripped away, we may continue to see normal members of our species as possessing greater capacities of rationality, self-consciousness, communication, and so on, than members of any other species; but we will not regard as sacrosanct the life of each and every member of our species, no matter how limited his capacity for intelligent or even conscious life may be. If we compare a severely defective human infant with a non-human animal, a dog or a pig for example, we will often find the non-human to have superior capacities, both actual and potential, for rationality, self-consciousness, communication, and anything else that can be plausibly considered morally significant.

Far from Peter Singer and company being in jest, this view, while somewhat more brutally expressed than usual, represents the majority opinion of biomedical ethicists in America today. For instance, see the work done by Joseph Fletcher, particularly his book *Humanhood.*

24. A sample of the many fine titles, journals, magazines, and periodicals written from a strongly prolife and well-informed point of view would include *Fighting for Life* by Melinda Delahoyde (Ann Arbor, MI: Servant Books); *Justice for the Unborn* by Judge Randall Hekman (Ann Arbor, MI: Servant Books); *The Death Decision* by Leonard J. Nelson (Ann Arbor, MI: Servant Books); *Abortion and the Conscience of the Nation* by Ronald R. Reagan, President of the United States (Nashville: Thomas Nelson Publishers); *Whatever Happened to the Human Race?* by Dr. C. Everett Koop and Francis Schaeffer (Westchester, IL: Crossway Books); *Abortion, the Silent Holocaust* by John Powell (Allen, TX: Argus Communications); *Single Issues* by Joseph Sobran (New York: The Human Life Foundation); *A Private Choice* by John T. Noonan (New York: The Free Press, Macmillan); *Rachael Weeping* by James Tunstead Burtchaell (Fairway, KS: Andrews and MacMeel); *The Rites of Life: The Scientific Evidence for Life Before Birth* by Landrum Shettles and David Rorvik (Grand Rapids, MI: Zondervan, 1983). Journals such as *The Human Life Review,* 150 E. 35th Street, New York, NY 10016, have, since 1973, covered on a regular basis the whole range of human life issues. Public figures such as Dr. C. Everett Koop, Francis A. Schaeffer, John Whitehead, Franky Schaeffer, Archbishop Bernard Law, and many others have routinely spoken out on the issue. Film series such as *Whatever Happened to the Human Race?, Conceived in Liberty, The Great Evangelical Disaster,* and many filmstrips have also been produced.

25. Take for example, Allan Johnson, professor of ethics at Wheaton College. First, it is interesting to note his priorities. In a recent course on ethics he devoted three classes to world hunger and the Third World, the remainder on a number of other topics. Only one was dedicated to the

question of human life and abortion. In that class, the focus of attention was first to establish that Christians could allow abortion for "therapeutic" reasons (a la Carl F. H. Henry, etc.), and the rest of the class was then centered around finding what these "therapeutic" abortions could be. What exceptions to the rule of protecting unborn life could Christians find? Such questions as the facts that only 3 percent or less of all abortions performed are for reasons of the life of the mother, rape, or incest were not mentioned. The fact that of the 1.5 million abortions performed a year, more and more are performed later and later term, via amniocentesis, the very method by which one finds handicapped children and then "therapeutically" aborts them, was never mentioned. It is interesting to note that the evangelical establishment, Wheaton College being prominent in it, has taken so little time to discuss the actual evil of abortion, and now spends whatever time they do allot to abortion to delve into the subject in finding *excuses* on why we ought to allow abortions in some extreme cases. Such thinking and such "ethics" mock the idea that Christian values should inform every area of life in a way that secular values do not. The very words *absolute, right,* and *wrong* take on a meaningless aura of a mirage, and ethics finally boil down to classroom discussion on how you *feel* about something.

26. See Footnote 22.

27. For instance, in the 1984 Presidential campaign Geraldine Ferraro was quoted on this subject. " 'My religion is a very private thing,' she said . . . insisting that conservative groups had questioned her religious belief because of her views on abortion. 'How I vote on things shouldn't bring into question whether or not I'm a good Catholic.' " *Wall Street Journal,* July 19, 1984. This is just one of many instances showing that in her mind being a "good Catholic" has nothing to do with and did not contradict her public stand on "abortion rights."

28. See "Our Reich of Indifference" by Joseph Bayly, published in *Eternity,* June 1984. Bayly accuses the evangelical establishment of complicity and indifference in the matter of abortion.

29. It is interesting to note that far from *Christianity Today* standing against the views on abortion espoused by Carl Henry, they have rewarded him by hiring him as a special editor, at the end of 1984.

30. In a list of endorsements printed by InterVarsity Press and handed out at the 1984 Christian Booksellers Association Convention, Arthur Holmes was quoted as saying, *"Brave New People* is a thoughtful treatment of complex moral problems in modern medicine. InterVarsity Press has continued its long-standing contribution to a careful Christian discussion of matters over which evangelicals disagree."￼ In addition, Arthur Holmes has been credited with endorsing the book before its publication and thus assisting in leading InterVarsity Press to make the decision to publish the book.

31. Germaine Greer, in her new book *Sex and Destiny* (New York: Harper & Row, 1984), details the rise of the eugenic movement mentality in the world population control efforts of Planned Parenthood and other zealous secularist institutions. This is particularly instructive since Germaine Greer was a preeminent feminist who did a great deal to open the door to legalized abortion in the first place. While she has not changed her mind on the "right" of women to seek abortions, she nevertheless exposes the fradulent, coercive wickedness of the worldwide pro-death movement, usually called population planning.

32. See the essay by novelist Harold Fickett, also an ex-Wheaton College professor, entitled "Coming Out," in the January issue of *The Christian Activist* newspaper, published by Schaeffer Productions, P. O. Box 909, Los Gatos, CA.

33. The "I'm personally opposed, but . . ." position has been espoused by numerous political leaders, including Geraldine Ferraro. It has also been espoused by various evangelical leaders, including Richard Halverson, Senate Chaplain. In a *Christianity Today* interview, November 12, 1982, Halverson was asked to respond to the fact that some Christians were not standing against abortion and indeed supported it. He said, "It's just very difficult; I don't really know the answers. Perhaps part of the expla-

nation is that all of us hear God's truth a little differently. We hear it in terms of the way we are made, our backgrounds, our genes. The result is that the body of Christ is very diverse. And I suppose there is a sense in which we have to honor individualism within the church." Halverson's ambivalence was reconfirmed in a *Washington Post* interview, August 3, 1983, in which he said, "I would say right away that I oppose abortion, but I also believe very strongly that God has endowed us with free-will and the responsibility for free choice." The *Post* in the editorial note after the interview also noted that Halverson had "no desire to influence legislation." His views were confirmed by the *Presbyterian Journal* in a personal interview with the editor in reference to confirming this author's allegations.

Chapter Three: Violence and the Prolife Movement

1. Alma Guillermoprieto, "Pro-Abortion Organizations Protest Growing Violence Against Facilities," *Washington Post* (July 7, 1984), p. 85.
2. Abe Fortas, "Concerning Dissent and Civil Disobedience" (1968), p. 24.
3. Jean-Paul Sartre, *Being and Nothingness* (New York: Philosophical Library, 1956), p. 566.
4. Walter Odajnyk, *Marxism and Existentialism* (1965), p. 99.
5. *Ibid.*, p. 13.
6. Os Guinness, *The Dust of Death* (Downers Grove, IL: InterVarsity Press), p. 173.
7. Albert Camus, *The Rebel* (New York: Alfred A. Knopf, 1962), p. 146.
8. George Orwell, *1984* (New York: Harcourt Brace Jovanovich, 1950), p. 203.
9. Harold O. J. Brown, *The Reconstruction of the Republic* (Milford, MI: Mott Media, 1977), pp. 132-137.
10. 372 U.S. 229 (1963).
11. *Ibid.*, p. 235.
12. *Ibid.*, pp. 230-231.
13. *Ibid.*, p. 236 (emphasis added)
14. *Ibid.*, p. 235.

15. Frantz Fanon, *The Wretched of the Earth* (New York: Grove, 1967), p. 74.

Chapter Four: Infanticide

1. Anne Brannon, *The Case of the Bloomington Baby,* 8 *Human Life Review* 60 (Fall 1982).
2. Richard H. Gross, M.D., et al, "Early Management and Decision-Making for the Treatment of Myclomeningoiele," *Pediatrics,* Volume 72, Number 4 (October 1983), pp. 450-458.
3. Peter Singer, "Sanctity of Life or Quality of Life?" *Pediatrics,* Volume 72, Number 1 (July 1983), pp. 128, 129.
4. Raymond S. Huff and A. G. M. Campbell, "Moral and Ethical Dilemnas in the Special Care Nursery," *New England Journal of Medicine,* Volume 289 (1973), pp. 890-894.
5. *Ibid.*

About the Authors

Melinda Delahoyde
Melinda Delahoyde was a veteran participant in the pro-life movement when she began to concentrate on investigating the medical and legal maltreatment of newborns considered "unworthy" of life. She is now widely known among prolifers for her documented exposés on the growing acceptance and practice of infanticide and the devastating trend to devalue the lives of handicapped children. Her interest in this latter issue was strengthened after the birth of her son Will, who has Down's syndrome.

Seeking to educate Christians on these trends and move them to effective counteraction, Mrs. Delahoyde has written two books: *Fighting for Life: Defending the Newborn's Right to Life* and *Infanticide and the Handicapped Newborn* (coauthored). In addition, her articles have appeared in Christian magazines such as *Moody Monthly* and *Christian Life*. Mrs. Delahoyde has appeared on numerous national and local radio and television programs, including "The 700 Club" and Dr. James Dobson's "Focus on the Family."

She is a member of the board of directors of the Christian Action Council, the largest Protestant prolife organization in the United States. She is also a former director of education for Americans United for Life.

Address: Mrs. Melinda Delahoyde, 809 Buckle Court, Raleigh, NC 27609.

D. James Kennedy

Dr. D. James Kennedy, pastor of Coral Ridge Presbyterian Church in Ft. Lauderdale, Florida, has guided his congregation from its original fledgling group of seventeen to its current membership of more than five thousand. He is now recognized nationwide as a leading Christian statesman, with a straightforward and practical approach to teaching God's Word.

Dr. Kennedy won national prominence through his landmark book *Evangelism Explosion,* which is now used throughout the United States and in fifty other nations to equip Christians with a successful, versatile lay witness program that crosses denominational lines. Other writings by Dr. Kennedy include *Why I Believe, Truths That Transform,* and *The God of Great Surprises.*

Dr. Kennedy is a much-in-demand speaker for various Christian groups and events, and his weekly television broadcast is one of the top-ranked evangelistic programs in the United States.

Dr. Kennedy holds a Doctor of Divinity degree from Trinity Evangelical School and a Ph.D. from New York University.

Address: Coral Ridge Ministries, P. O. Box 5555, Ft. Lauderdale, FL 33310.

Marilyn Lewis

The daughter of Dr. and Mrs. Al Metsker, founders of Kansas City Youth for Christ, Mrs. Marilyn Lewis has been personally active in that ministry for many years. Eight years ago she spearheaded a volunteer organization called the Women's March for Christian Television, which launched a successful two-year fund-raising effort to establish a local Youth for Christ television station.

Mrs. Lewis's husband, David, now serves as general manager of TV-50.

Concerned that many Christians were ill-informed about important contemporary issues—particularly those affecting their children—Mrs. Lewis began hosting "Vibrations," a weekly television program that addressed many of those issues from a Christian perspective. She continues to conduct TV interviews with various individuals, and has become a popular speaker in her own right.

In addition to her other Youth for Christ activities, Mrs. Lewis started the LIGHT House as a Christian resource to women and girls facing crisis pregnancies. The LIGHT House provides shelter, physical care, job training, and spiritual counseling at no cost to the women.

Address: Kansas City Youth for Christ, 4715 Rainbow Boulevard, Shawnee Mission, KS 66205.

David N. O'Steen and Darla St. Martin

David N. O'Steen, Ph.D., and Darla St. Martin serve as executive director and associate executive director respectively of the National Right-To-Life Committee, Inc. The NRLC encompasses more than two thousand local prolife groups nationwide, working for passage of prolife legislation that will reverse the growth of abortion on demand sanctioned by the Supreme Court's *Roe v. Wade* decision. The NRLC promotes respect for all human life through legal defense and lobby efforts, research, educational seminars and materials, and media communications. The NRLC Political Action Committee supports prolife candidates for federal office and encourages active prolife participation in the American political process.

Dr. O'Steen and Mrs. St. Martin have also served as co-directors of the Committee for a Pro-Life Congress, set up to help elect prolife candidates. Both have traveled extensively throughout the United States as consultants on prolife organizational development and political issues.

Address: National Right-To-Life Committee, Suite 402, 419 7th Street N.W., Washington, DC 20004.

Franky Schaeffer
Franky Schaeffer has been an outspoken defender of the sanctity of human life for many years. As founder and president of Schaeffer V Productions, he has been awarded substantial credit from prolifers for alerting Christians to the increased practice of abortion, infanticide, and euthanasia. Mr. Schaeffer's jarring film series *Whatever Happened to the Human Race?* has been viewed by hundreds of thousands of people throughout the United States, and a modified version was broadcast during prime time on an ABC affiliate.

Schaeffer V Productions also produced the award-winning series *How Should We Then Live?; The Second American Revolution;* and *The Great Evangelical Disaster.* This newest film, an animated "political cartoon," uses satire and caricature to forcefully depict the growth of secularism and to drive Christians to moral outrage and action.

In addition to its hard-hitting films to educate and motivate Christians, the company also produces a quarterly newspaper, *The Christian Activist,* with a present circulation of over one hundred thousand.

Because of his unflinching defense of the value of human life, Mr. Schaeffer has been a frequent keynote speaker at prolife conferences and rallies throughout the country. He has written four books: *Addicted to Mediocrity, A Time for Anger, Bad News for Modern Man,* and *A Modest Proposal.* The third book is a call for Christians to *fight* the secular onslaught that has spawned the brutalization of human life and the destruction of our nation's moral foundations.

Address: Schaeffer V Productions, Box 909, Los Gatos, CA 95030.

Joseph Scheidler

Joseph Scheidler is the executive director of the Pro-Life Action League, a national educational organization that capitalizes on the media to expose the facts about abortion.

National syndicated columnist Patrick Buchanan has called Mr. Scheidler one of the prolife movement's "Green Berets" because of his many campaigns against Planned Parenthood and other agencies promoting abortion.

Convinced that it would take the interest of the *secular* press to rouse public concern for the deplorable conditions of Chicago's abortion clinics, Mr. Scheidler instigated an undercover investigation by the Chicago *Sun-Times*. The newspaper's resulting twenty-one-part exposé, "The Abortion Profiteers," helped shut down six clinics in Chicago and led to the two-year imprisonment of one abortionist. The series also contributed to the passage of more restrictive abortion legislation in Illinois as well as in several other states.

Mr. Scheidler has appeared on more than five hundred radio and television programs, including "ABC News Nightline," "The MacNeil/Lehrer Report," and the "Donahue" show.

In addition to his many newspaper and magazine articles, Mr. Scheidler recently completed a book entitled *Closed: 99 Ways to Stop Abortion*.

Prior to his current position, he wrote for the *South Bend Tribune*, taught journalism and speech at the University of Notre Dame, and taught journalism at Chicago's Mundelein College.

Address: Pro-Life Action League, 6160 N. Cicero Avenue, Suite 210, Chicago, IL 60646.

John W. Whitehead
John Whitehead is recognized as one of America's top constitutional attorneys, specializing in religious freedom. In 1982 he founded the Rutherford Institute to aggressively defend the First Amendment rights of religious persons threatened by state action and to educate the Christian community on issues of great import. He now serves as president and chairman of the board of the Virginia-based organization.

As an attorney, Mr. Whitehead considers his number one priority the defense of the sanctity of all human life. This commitment is reflected in the caseload of the Rutherford Institute, which has defended several people whose courageous campaigns against abortion led to arrest or burdensome lawsuits.

Mr. Whitehead has traveled extensively as a speaker, alerting Christians to the growing secularization of the courts and the disturbing aftermath of the *Roe v. Wade* ruling that legalized abortion on demand. He has also been interviewed on numerous radio and television programs, including "The 700 Club."

A prolific writer, Mr. Whitehead is highly regarded for his painstakingly researched and documented analyses of America's legal system and its decaying moral foundations. He has written nine books, including: *The Second American Revolution; The Stealing of America; The Freedom of Religious Expression in the Public High Schools; Home Education and Constitutional Liberties; The Right to Picket and the Freedom of Public Discourse;* and *The End of Man.* A film version of *The Second American Revolution,* produced by Schaeffer V Productions, has met with nationwide acclaim among churches and conservative groups. Special showings of the film were also held in the White House and on Capitol Hill.

Address: The Rutherford Institute, P.O. Box 510, Manassas, VA 22110.

The Rutherford Institute

The Rutherford Institute is a Virginia-based legal and educational organization that upholds the sanctity of human life and defends persons whose First Amendment religious liberties are threatened by state action.

The Institute has proved to be a valuable resource to prolife groups through its aggressive defense of abortion protestors who have been arrested or become embroiled in costly lawsuits.

Institute attorneys successfully defended James and David Henderson, who were sued for $200,000 after they picketed an abortion clinic in Jacksonville, North Carolina. On their placards and picketing application, the brothers referred to the abortionists as "baby slayers," "sadistic and money-hungry butchers," and other equally candid descriptions. Physicians at the clinic, known to abort eight to ten unborn children every day, sued the Hendersons for slander, libel, and defamation.

Institute attorneys countered with arguments that the brothers were lawfully exercising their First Amendment right to freedom of speech. A Superior Court judge ruled in the Hendersons' favor, confirming that the message constituted *protected* speech.

In another case that ended successfully for prolifers, Institute attorneys assisted in the defense of members of Rock Church in Virginia Beach, Virginia, and North Carolina Right to Life. They faced both criminal charges and lawsuits after picketing an abortion clinic in Norfolk, Virginia.

Once contacted for assistance, Institute attorneys launched aggressive legal action, arguing on behalf of the demonstrators' First Amendment rights and filing a counterclaim against the clinic for harassment and violation of the Constitution. The actions proved successful:

all of the criminal cases and lawsuits were dismissed when the court upheld the picketers' right to express their moral and religious views within broad guidelines.

The Institute also participated in the defense of Robin DeMaggio, a young evangelist arrested for criminal trespass after he knelt to pray in front of a New York abortion clinic. In the first round of legal action, DeMaggio was convicted by a Criminal Court Judge who refused to consider the "justification defense" raised by Institute attorneys. The Institute argued that DeMaggio was justified in his actions because he was trying to *save* human lives. The judge stated, however, that allowing the justification defense would be "an embracement of tyranny and anarchy" because it would essentially overturn the Supreme Court's legalization of abortion. The case is now on appeal.

In addition to cases related to abortion and the protection of human life, the Institute is committed to defending parental liberty and responsibility (particularly in the area of home education), the freedoms of religious expression and speech in public places, and the right of the church to operate free from state intrusion.

To educate the public on these priority issues, the Institute publishes numerous books and papers, and makes available legal briefs to assist attorneys involved in similar litigation.

To make its services more accessible, the Institute is establishing a network of state chapters, with the goal to have at least one chapter in each of the fifty states.

Address: The Rutherford Institute, P.O. Box 510, Manassas, VA 22110.